BestMasters

Springer awards "BestMasters" to the best application-oriented master's theses, which were completed at renowned chairs of economic sciences in Germany, Austria, and Switzerland in 2013.

The works received highest marks and were recommended for publication by supervisors. As a rule, they show a high degree of application orientation and deal with current issues from different fields of economics.

The series addresses practitioners as well as scientists and offers guidance for early stage researchers.

Olga Louisa Kastner

When Luxury Meets Art

Forms of Collaboration between Luxury Brands and the Arts

With a foreword by Prof. Dr. Carsten Baumgarth

Springer Gabler

Olga Louisa Kastner
Berlin, Germany

OnlinePLUS Material to this book can be downloaded from
http://www.springer-gabler.de/978-3-658-04575-3

ISBN 978-3-658-04575-3 ISBN 978-3-658-04576-0 (eBook)
DOI 10.1007/978-3-658-04576-0

The Deutsche Nationalbibliothek lists this publication in the Deutsche Nationalbibliografie; detailed bibliographic data are available in the Internet at http://dnb.d-nb.de.

Library of Congress Control Number: 2013955736

Springer Gabler

Printed on acid-free paper

Springer Gabler is a brand of Springer DE.
Springer DE is part of Springer Science+Business Media.
www.springer-gabler.de

Geleitwort

Kunst und Wirtschaft könnte eines der kommenden Top-Themen der Management- und Markenforschung sowie der Unternehmenspraxis werden. Dies belegt eine Vielzahl von aktuellen Beispielen in der Unternehmenspraxis, eine verstärkte Forschungsintensität und auch erste Ansätze zur Integration von Kunst in die Managementausbildung an Hochschulen weltweit.

Die Schnittstelle von Kunst und Wirtschaft umfasst dabei ein breites Spektrum: Einsatz von künstlerischen Techniken im Rahmen der Organisations- und Personalentwicklung, Sponsoring von Kunst und Kultur, Gestaltung von Arbeitsumgebungen durch Künstler und Kunst, Integration von Kunstwerken und Künstlern in die Marketingkommunikation oder Angebot von kunstbezogenen Limited Editions. Grundsätzlich lassen sich bei solchen Kunst-Unternehmens-Kooperationen (KUK) durch die Wirkungsrichtung interne und externe Formen als zwei Grundtypen unterscheiden. Die vorliegende Masterarbeit von Frau Olga Louisa Kastner, die den Einsatz solcher KUKs im Rahmen der Markenführung von Luxusmarken untersucht, ist der zweiten Form zuzuordnen.

Dabei stellen Luxusmarken ein ideales Untersuchungsgebiet dar, weil speziell Luxusmarken schon seit Jahren solche Kollaborationen mit Kunst einsetzen und damit auch als Vorreiter und Vorbild für viele weitere Branchen dienen können. Die hohe praktische Bedeutung belegt auch die vorliegende Masterarbeit, die empirisch bestimmt hat, dass rund 16 % aller Luxusmarken weltweit aktuell oder in der jüngsten Vergangenheit in der Markenführung nach außen sichtbar mit Kunst kooperieren.

Die Arbeit von Frau Kastner stellt einen ersten theoretischen und empirischen Ansatz zur Analyse dieser Option der Markenführung dar und bildet damit einen Meilenstein zur systematischen Erfassung dieses Phänomens. Dabei entwickelt die Arbeit zunächst auf der Basis der Literatur und ausgewählten Fallbeispielen einen Katalog mit insgesamt 23 Merkmalen zur Beschreibung solcher KUKs. Dieser Katalog dient als Grundlage zur Entwicklung einer empirisch gestützten Realtypologie. Dazu werden insgesamt über 130 Kooperationen von Luxusmarken mit Kunst identifiziert und anhand ausgewählter Merkmale beschrieben. Eine anschließende Clusteranalyse ergab mit „Arty Limited Editions“, „Philanthropic Luxury-Brand-Art Collaborations“ und „Experimental Luxury-Brand-Art Collaboration“ drei abgrenzbare Typen, die abschließend mit jeweils einem Fallbeispiel illustriert wurden.

Die gefundenen Typen zeigen die Heterogenität dieser Option auf, verdeutlichen dem Manager die grundsätzlichen Möglichkeiten und dienen dem Forscher als Ausgangspunkt für differenzierte Analysen von Erfolgsfaktoren oder Wirkungsstudien differenziert nach diesen drei grundsätzlichen Typen. Weiterhin erscheinen die identifizierten Typen sowie der gewählte methodische Ansatz grundsätzlich geeignet, um KUKs auch in anderen Branchen wie z. B. Mode, Fast Moving Consumer Goods oder Dienstleistungen zu analysieren.

In Anbetracht des bisher geringen Forschungsstandes, der zunehmenden Bedeutung des Themas in der Praxis und Wissenschaft sowie der hohen inhaltlichen und methodischen Qualität der Arbeit ist der Masterarbeit eine weite Verbreitung zu wünschen.

Berlin, 1.9.2013

Prof. Dr. Carsten Baumgarth
Professur für Marketing, insbesondere Markenführung
Fachgebiet: Marketing
Hochschule für Wirtschaft und Recht, Berlin

Acknowledgements

My special thanks go to Professor Carsten Baumgarth for his mentoring and support throughout the research process. I also wish to thank Dr. Klaus Heine for his permission to access the 'World Luxury Brand Directory', which has substantially facilitated the empirical data collection.

"Artists incarnate the idea of the unique and the rare,
which is the very foundation of luxury."
(Fabrice Hyber, French artist)

Table of contents

List of figures

List of tables

A. Introduction

1. Topicality and practical relevance of the research question

Ever more luxury brands join forces with the arts today (Lieblich, 2013). Yet, these cross-over collaborations do not constitute a homogenous strategy, but become manifest in manifold forms and appearances. Both the heterogeneity and high relevance of this interdisciplinary approach are illustrated by numerous real-life examples. To name but a few, the diamond manufacturer *De Beers* commissioned conceptual artist Rolf Sachs to create a window installation for the brand's 2012 Christmas season (McKay, 2012), while hybrid artist Vanessa Beecroft staged an experimental performance at the opening event of the *Louis Vuitton* flagship store on the Champs-Élysées in Paris (LaBoulbenne, 2005). Likewise, the French fashion house *Christian Dior* asked visual artist Anselm Reyle to reinvent the label's most iconic handbags with the objective of launching an exclusive limited edition collection (Marandon, 2011), while the high-end jeweller *Cartier* has succeeded, with its Paris-based art foundation, in establishing a renowned museum for contemporary art. Similarly, the Italian fashion label *MaxMara* has dedicated itself to support female artists that have made significant contributions to the contemporary art scene by awarding the "MaxMara Art Prize for Women" (O'Donovan, 2011), while the luxury goods company *Bulgari* has been sponsoring for many years now the discussion platform "Art Basel Conversations" with a view to bringing together leading personalities from the art world and letting them debate on the current state of the artistic mindset (Petersen, 2008). – The collectivity of these examples can be generally coined as "Luxury Brand-Art Collaborations" and are hereinafter shortly referred to as LBACs.

In the literature, the "current love affair" (Michau, 2009) between luxury and art is ascribed to the "structural proximity" between both concepts (Kapferer/Bastien, 2012, p. 107) and a number of key challenges that the luxury industry has been facing for some time past.

On the one hand, luxury brands and the arts are often mentioned in one breath since they tend to occur in similar (social) contexts and function according to analogue principles: First, both concepts refer to a highly coded, visual language (Petersen, 2008). Secondly, the practical utility of both concepts is usually of secondary importance and translates into an actual use-value that frequently equals zero, but into a very high symbolic value for the consumer (Kapferer/Bastien, 2012, p. 32). Thirdly, as both luxury goods and works of art are commonly sold at extraordinarily high prices, both industries cater to the wealth of the world's richest customers in order to fuel profits at the top end of the market (Burns, 2012). As a result, both concepts serve as powerful means of distinction and strong social markers that bestow upon their consumers status, prestige and high levels of attention within their reference groups (Adlwarth, 1983, p. 49ff.; Lasslop, 2005, p. 475; Petersen, 2008). By collaborating, both concepts reinforce each other, further fortify their eminent position in society and effectively perpetuate the "social hierarchy" (Marraro, 2012).

On the other hand, teaming up with the arts appears, at least partially, to be an effective strategy to deal with a series of difficulties that luxury brands have long been searching expedient solutions for. While the luxury market had traditionally been deemed largely untroubled by competitive threats such as high levels of rivalry, intense price pressures or short innovation cycles (Lasslop, 2005, p. 471), the "democratization of luxury" (Kennedy, 2010, p. 2) in the wake of both "trading-up" strategies pursued by so-called "masstige" brands (Silverstein/Fiske, 2005, p. 1ff.) and "downwards" marketing activities followed by an increasing number of luxury brands (Kapferer/Bastien, 2012, p. 43), has lately entailed both a substantial rise in competition and considerable danger to the typically exclusive positioning of the luxury brand. Yet, luxury brands also need to "chase sales" and expand into new markets in order to amortise their ever-growing communication and distribution costs (Catry, 2003, p. 11). As a result, luxury brands are nowadays exposed to stronger pressures to innovate and must continuously seek for new ways to stand out from the crowd (Lasslop, 2005, p. 471; similar: Bruce/Kratz, 2007, p. 133ff.). The latter challenge is all the more critical since luxury brands are usually associated with rather conservative values such as tradition, heritage and timelessness and must thus fight even harder in order to be perceived as bold and original brand personalities (Kapferer/Bastien, 2012, p. 34). Changing social norms finally oblige luxury brands to take part in societal debates, commit to good causes and "demonstrate a clear conscience" (Kennedy, 2010, p. 3).

Against this background, joining forces with the arts offers several opportunities. As a counter-measure against the current up- and down-trading tendencies, art collaborations help luxury brands to regain their lost distance towards competing (masstige) brands and non-targeted "middle-market" customers (Silverstein/Fiske, 2005, p. 1) by building on the strong social demarcation function of art (Petersen, 2008). Hence, since the art world is commonly not readily accessible for the average consumer, luxury brands, by entering the artistic sphere, affirm their distinctive connoisseurship and emphasise their belonging to elitist networks (Meffert/Lasslop, 2004, p. 940). In this way, luxury brands re-nourish their exclusive image and alleged (since only artificially) scarce character (Catry, 2003, p. 13). Moreover, by tapping into the arts' creativity, luxury brands manage to remain inventive, access new innovative capacity and surprise their demanding target clientele with eclectic marketing initiatives (Klanten/Ehmann/Sinofzik, 2012, p. 4ff.). Entering high-profile collaborations with the art world thus represents one of the easiest ways for luxury brands to communicate their aspirational messages and to guarantee a wide range of media exposure (Michau, 2009). At the same time, showing interest in domestic cultures and local art scenes often permits luxury brands to enter foreign markets and to woo new customers (Maxwell, 2011). Besides, especially the forward-thinking contemporary arts enable luxury brands to reconnect with the zeitgeist, rejuvenate and assert their sense of modernity (Barron, 2012). Through their commitment to the intangible arts, luxury brands finally prove that their scope is not solely self-referential or purely commercial, but also encompasses cultural concerns and even "intellectual high ground" (Foulkes, 2009).

2. Problem definition and course of the investigation

While the above examples both demonstrate the widespread popularity and recurrent use of LBACs in the international luxury goods industry and illustrate the strategic potential of these collaborations for the practical challenges of contemporary luxury branding, so far, the issue of LBACs has been largely overlooked by the academic discourse.

Even though various standard works on luxury brand management have dedicated entire chapters to the relationship between luxury and art (e.g. Chevalier/Mazzalovo, 2012, p. 208ff.; Kapferer/Bastien, 2012, p. 32ff., p. 78 and p. 107ff.; Tungate, 2009, p. 105ff.), they focus virtually exclusively on the historic parallels and conceptual proximity between both notions. They thereby forego analysing LBACs as an independent strategy for which it would be worth identifying distinct types of collaboration[1], major dimensions of success or critical success factors. Likewise, the repeated phenomenon of LBACs has been only marginally dealt with in scientific publications. If single forms of LBACs are discussed, they never represent the core topic of the article, but are typically solely cited as one illustrating example of a larger marketing or branding practice (e.g. Catry, 2003; Dion/Arnould, 2011). Neither concentrate these publications on the appearance of art in the scope of luxury brands, but rather explore the beneficial impact of art across all conceivable industries,

1 The only existing classification approach to date considers solely two organising dimensions and refers exclusively to theoretical assumptions (Chevalier/Mazzalovo 2012, p. 209).

categories and corporate functions, with individual forms of LBACs serving merely as one specific case in point (e.g. Schwaiger/Sarstedt/Taylor, 2010).

The lack of attention given to LBACs within the scientific community can potentially be ascribed to three main reasons. First, due to the conceptual proximity between luxury goods and works of art and the further convergence between the latter through the ongoing heavy commercialisation of the international art market[2] (Graw, 2008; similar: Chevalier/Mazzalovo, 2012, p. 212ff.), there is a tendency to perceive the idea of luxury and that of art as either inseparable or interchangeable concepts (Kapferer/ Bastien, 2012, p. 32). As a result, one might be tempted to assume that both concepts, since they are obviously so close to each other, would logically regularly join forces and to treat, hence, the occurrence of LBACs as irrelevant (Petersen, 2008). Secondly, the close alliances between luxury brands and the arts, as they can be empirically observed today, represent a quite young phenomenon (Michau, 2009) that has only been effectively triggered in 2004 when *Louis Vuitton* launched, under the creative direction of Marc Jacobs, a highly publicised limited edition bag designed by the Japanese pop art artist Takashi Murakami (Maxwell, 2011). The practice of LBACs accordingly has a relatively short tradition in the field of luxury brand management and is still in the process of exploring further opportunities for its implementation (Boche, 2010). Thirdly, owing to the myriad manifestations of LBACs, until now, no uniform terminology has emerged that would cover all empirically observable forms of LBACs and simultaneously refer to a specified underlying strategy or clear-cut concept[3].

Regardless of their increasing practical relevance for the creation of contemporary luxury brands, the varied forms of LBACs have thus remained widely unexplored to date. The present thesis sets in at this point: Seeking to provide first substantial insights into the heterogeneous strategy of LBACs, the aim of this work is to systematise the different collaborative patterns between luxury brands and the arts by empirically deriving, based on methodically developed attributes, distinct types of

2 The process of commercialisation of the contemporary art market has been taken so far lately that the prices for works of art can no longer be rationally understood, and that high-profile artists such as Damien Hirst are themselves regarded as brands (Tungate, 2009, p. 111ff.; similar: Chevalier/Mazzalovo, 2012, p. 212) – and even as "luxury brand[s]" (Farago, 2012).

3 The only initiative in this regard represents the approach by the French brand strategist Boche (2010) who, in an often-quoted blog post, has coined the term "Artketing" in order to address the collaborations between luxury brands and art (cf. B.3.2). Yet, this notion is not adhered to in the context of this thesis since it neither explicitly hints at the involvement of luxury brands nor covers the myriad forms of collaboration that this thesis aims at merging into distinct types.

LBACs. To this end, the following investigation will comprise three main parts that are briefly outlined below.

(1) Theoretical foundations: As the concept of LBACs is composed of two constituent parts (the luxury brand on the one, and the arts on the other hand), it will initially be necessary to define the latter notions in greater detail. In this regard, close attention will be paid to the issue of how to best operationalise the abstract idea of art for the empirical purposes of this study. Once the theoretical foundations are laid, the composite concept of LBACs can be addressed by providing a short overview of its historical evolution, discussing existing literature approaches, developing an autonomous definition of LBACs and, based on the latter, demarcating the practice of LBACs from related concepts.

(2) Conceptual framework: In order to merge the manifold forms of LBACs into distinct types, attributes must first be derived that best describe the phenomenon of LBACs in its diverse manifestations. With a view to detecting these attributes, a dual, namely deductive-inductive approach will be followed. On the one hand, related fields of research are examined for attributes that may prove useful for characterising LBACs. In this regard, special attention will be paid to the relevant literature in the areas of luxury brand management, brand leveraging, interfirm co-operation and art-business management. On the other hand, selected case studies are briefly analysed in order to derive attributes that would, due to the mostly uncharted scope and interdisciplinary composition of LBACs, possibly not be identified if one pursued exclusively a deductive approach.

(3) Empirical-quantitative study: With the objective of incorporating within the typological study as many real cases of LBACs as possible, all luxury brands from a comprehensive, pre-existing database will be tested for potential collaborations with the arts. The detected LBACs are subsequently described by the attributes that have been previously derived and, based on a cluster analysis performed via the software package for statistical analyses SPSS, grouped into distinct types of LBACs. In order to provide the latter with a tangible profile, they will eventually be explained in their dominating characteristic values, given a visual name and further illustrated by prototypical cases.

The last chapter finally discusses both the benefits and limitations of the typological study.

B. Basics

1. Explanations on the notion of the luxury brand

Since antiquity, myriad studies in economics, consumer research and sociology have been trying to define the notions of luxury, luxury good and luxury brand (Valtin, 2005, p. 19). Yet, to date, no universally valid, overarching definition exists (Vickers/ Renand, 2003, p. 461). In the following, the goal is thus to provide a deeper understanding of both the etymological complexity and historic ambivalence of the concept of luxury, to discuss dominant approaches to defining the term of the luxury brand and to give a succinct overview on the latter's functions and effects on the consumer.

1.1 Notion, history and definition of the concept of luxury

Etymologically, the word luxury derives from the Latin word 'lux' and can be translated as light, luminosity or luminance, thereby referring to the outer radiance of luxury objects. This derivation does not only explain the common use of precious materials such as gold, gems and diamonds within the manufacturing process of luxury items, but also hints at the latter's characteristic conspicuousness and external visibility (Kapferer, 2001, p. 349). On the other hand, the word luxury stems from the Latin words 'luxus' and 'luxuria' whose meaning can be considered as roughly the same since both allude to the **deviation from the normal respectively the standard** (Grugel-Pannier, 1996, p. 17ff.; Mühlmann, 1975, p. 22). This derivation points to the latent judgement and subliminal critique that the concept of luxury is usually exposed to. The definition of what constitutes the standard appears to be **fundamentally normative** and might accordingly substantially differ among individuals depending on, amongst others, their particular value system or income situation (Jäckel/Kochhan, 2000, p. 75). Hence, while some consumers may consider luxury items as special products that clearly exceed their daily requirements, another set of consumers may take these same luxury products for granted by qualifying them as normal and constituent part of their everyday life (Kapferer, 2001, p. 347; Vigneron/Johnson 2004, p. 486). Likewise, while some consumers may regard luxury products as technically and/or aesthetically effective, superior and admirable, another set of consumers may condemn these same items as excessive, extravagant and useless (Kapferer, 2001, p. 347). Given that these perceptions are further impacted by personal attitudes, situational influences, politico-economical factors, temporal changes in society, cultural specificities or the product category (Büttner et al., 2006, p. 9; Jäckel/ Kochhan, 2000, p. 75ff.; Lasslop, 2005, p. 473; Phau/Prendergast, 2000, p. 122ff.;

Valtin, 2005, p. 20; Vukelic, 2000, p. 41; Wiedmann/Hennigs/Siebels, 2007), they provide evidence for the both **relative and subjective dimension of the concept of luxury** as well as for the **high degree of contextuality** when it comes to the attempt to define its meaning.

The perceived ambiguity towards the concept of luxury is also reflected in the historic interpretation of the term. Irrespective of the concrete definition of what represents the commonly accepted standard of living, from Ancient Greece to the 19th century, one can distinguish **two conflicting appraisals** as to the question on whether consumption patterns that exceed the subsistence minimum cause benefits or, in contrast, damages to society (Jäckel/Kochhan, 2000, p. 78ff.; Kapferer/Bastien, 2012, p. 7ff.). On the one hand, proponents qualified luxury as a revolutionary, improving and hence **aspirational force in human civilisation**, arguing that the ambition to luxury would help fostering the formation of the economic society (Jäckel/Kochhan, 2000, p. 79; Mandeville, 1957, p. 100ff.; Pallach, 1987, p. 138). On the other hand, critics declared luxury as the **adversary of all virtues and considerateness** and equated luxury rather with the idea of blindness than with that of light (Jäckel/Kochhan, 2000, p. 78; Kapferer/Bastien, 2012, p. 8).

Economic and social transformations as well as the Enlightenment Movement in the 18th century successively gave new meaning to the concept of luxury: Increased prosperity in the wake of the Industrial Revolution and the ongoing democratisation process made luxury both more accessible and acceptable to a broader public. Concurrently, leading English philosophers such as Adam Smith or David Hume stipulated the dissociation of luxury and morals, hitherto considered as mutually irreconcilable, if not even hostile ideologies in Christian Europe. Eventually, women's emancipation efforts throughout the 19th and 20th century further spurred the social legitimisation of luxury (Kapferer/Bastien, 2012, p. 9ff.). Yet, despite these societal upheavals, a uniform evaluation of the concept of luxury still did not become universally accepted at that stage. Criticism of the idea of luxury rather turned to be ever more differentiated (Valtin, 2005, p. 24). In this regard, the economic treatise "The Theory of the Leisure Class" by Thorstein Veblen has become a standard reference work and enjoys great popularity still today as one of the "most comprehensive" analyses of luxury in social sciences (Mortelmans, 2005, p. 497). Veblen (1934, p. 68ff.) argued that the ruling leisure class would use "conspicuous consumption" (defined as the publicly visible application of money and luxuries) to signal wealth and, by inference, power and status in deliberate demarcation from lower social strata.

Albeit being irreversible, the legitimisation process still does not appear to be finally completed in the industrial nations of the 21st century given that the concept of luxury interferes with three politically sensible topics: The persistence of social stratification, the idea of prodigality in an era of global resource shortages and the controversial issue of wealth distribution (Kapferer/Bastien, 2012, p. 8.).

Regardless of the persistently negative connotations of the idea of luxury, contemporary researchers usually take a more neutral approach and define the concept of luxury as a designation for **expenses that exceed the necessary**, that is, the commonly recognised and generally accepted minimum standard of living (Mühlmann, 1975, p. 69). Goods that are **dispensable to the satisfaction of one's basic needs** are accordingly considered as luxuries (Grugel-Pannier, 1996, p. 17; Sombart, 1967, p. 87).

1.2 Definition and conceptual demarcation of the luxury brand

The subjective quality of luxury has not only led to ambivalence among consumers, but has also entailed a large variety of heterogeneous approaches to defining the notion of the luxury brand[4] (Kapferer, 2006, p. 67ff.). Yet, a fundamental distinction is commonly drawn between the supply- or object-oriented rationale on the one, and the demand- or effect-oriented rationale on the other hand (Chevalier/Mazzalovo, 2012, p. 6ff.). Hereinafter, a selected overview on existing definitions of the luxury brand will be provided, systematised according to their chosen perspective and primary focus.

(1) Supply-oriented approach: Under the supply-oriented terminology, focus is put on the mechanisms of production and the functioning of luxury (Chevalier/Mazzalovo, 2012, p. 8). Accordingly, in contrast to "necessities" of everyday use (Bearden/Etzel, 1982, p. 184), luxury goods are characterised by less automated manufacturing processes, smaller production volumes, a superior product quality and higher price levels (Lasslop, 2005, p. 472). These product group features eventually translate into selective distribution policies, low levels of diffusion, artificial situations of scarcity and shortage and, therefore, high levels of exclusivity (Bearden/Etzel, 1982, p. 184).

While the idea of the luxury good thus serves to vertically distinguish between different product categories, the luxury brand horizontally signals the prominent position of marked products within one and the same product category (Lasslop, 2005, p. 473). To give but one example, as a result of mass production and generally

4 For detailed explanations of the basic concept of the brand see e.g. Bruhn (2004).

increased income levels, men's suits, wristwatches and automobiles recently tend to be counted rather among commodities than among luxury goods (Bearden/Etzel, 1982, p. 185). *Armani*, *Rolex* and *Rolls-Royce* are nonetheless qualified as luxury brands (Lasslop, 2005, p. 473).

Pursuant to the supply-driven rationale, equating the notion of the luxury good with that of the luxury brand entails that the classification of a brand primarily depends on the product category (Lasslop, 2005, p. 473). International brands such as *Dior*, *Prada* or *Chanel* can consequently be categorised as "griffe" for some part of their market activities, as "luxury brand" for another part of their business and as "upper-range brand" for a third part of their activities[5]. Conclusions as to the respective brand level are to be drawn according to supply-related criteria such as the manufacturing method, price, product quality, commercialisation approach, distribution policy and degree of diffusion (Kapferer, 2001, p. 352). In this regard, McKinsey (1990) puts special emphasis on the price/functionality ratio and defines those brands as luxury brands that succeed in the long term (at least five years) in charging a premium price, with the latter being a price that is substantially higher than that of products with comparable tangible functions[6]. Nueno/Quelch (1998, p. 62) take a similar approach by attributing special importance to both price and quality features, but extend the luxury brand's territory by a socio-psychological dimension: "Luxury brands are those whose ratio of functional utility to price is low while the ratio of intangible and situational utility to price is high". The latter definition paves the way for the demand-oriented perspective on the luxury brand.

(2) Demand-oriented approach: Under the demand-oriented terminology, the classification as a luxury brand is determined independently of the product category. Focus is rather put on the abstract brand core that serves as an overarching theme and is reflected in every product (Lasslop, 2005, p. 473). The latter idea refers to the concept of identity-oriented brand management (Burmann/Meffert, 2005) and has already been explicitly discussed in the area of luxury brand management by Dubois/ Paternault (1995, p. 71): "Whatever their nature and price, all products sold under the same brand name share a symbolic identity and a core of values expressing the 'quintessence' of the brand. Whether they are automobiles, wristwatches, writing instruments or sunglasses, all *Porsche* items express the *Porsche* 'legend' and are clearly identified as such". In this regard, Dubois/Laurent/Czellar (2001, p. 8ff.)

5 For a more detailed discussion on the originally quadripartite distinction between "griffe", "luxury brand", "upper-range brand" and "[generic] brand" see Kapferer (2001, p. 350ff.).

6 Tangible functions are defined as those product features that can be economically measured and contribute, along with the concrete product benefit, to the product quality (Kapferer, 2001, p. 348).

empirically identified six main facets that reflect the core of a luxury brand as subjectively perceived by the consumer and are today usually referred to as having imposed the prevailing definition of the luxury brand (de Barnier/Rodina/Vallette-Florence, 2006): **1. Excellent quality** (associated with the materials used, special diligence and high expertise within the manufacturing process), **2. Very high price** (referred to as absolute value of the price or by comparison with non-luxury alternatives within the same product category), **3. Scarcity and uniqueness** (reflected by restricted distribution channels and the categorical exclusion of mass-production), **4. Aesthetics and polysensuality** (entailing a profoundly hedonic shopping experience and multisensual consumption pleasure that is comparable to the study of a work of art), **5. Ancestral heritage and personal history** (mirrored in the luxury brand's anchoring in the past and reference to its founding legend on the one, and the consumer's individual experience with that brand on the other hand) and **6. Superfluousness** (equalling overabundance and translating into some kind of uselessness since luxury brands are not perceived as indispensable to one's physical survival).

Pursuant to a similar effect-oriented rationale, Vigneron/Johnson (1999) define the luxury brand as a function of the prestige criterion. Consumers would thus ascribe to "prestige brands" the capacity to satisfy their emotional desire for an outstanding aesthetic appeal, social recognition and a self-indulgent product experience. Interbrand (2008a, p. 3), in turn, bases its definition of the luxury brand exclusively on the latter's price positioning as perceived by the consumer. Accordingly, "a brand must 1. sit within a tier of a consumer-facing category that seemingly demonstrates price insensitivity; 2. show that being expensive is of neutral or even positive impact to their image; 3. demonstrate that perceived price has a low role among drivers of purchase". Since the modern understanding of the brand has shifted from a functional perspective to an identity- and thus primarily effect-oriented view (Meffert/Burmann, 2005), this thesis follows the demand-oriented approach to defining the luxury brand. Moreover, as the data collection required for the empirical purposes of this study will be based on the 'World Luxury Brand Directory' that was set up in 2011 by the expert for luxury brand marketing Heine (cf. D.2.1.2), the latter's effect-oriented definition will be adhered to under which

> "Luxury brands are regarded as images in the minds of consumers that comprise associations about a high level of price, quality, aesthetics, rarity, extraordinariness and a high degree of non-functional associations" (Heine, 2011, p. 46).

Yet, except for Kapferer's (2012, p. 70) quadripartite classification into "**griffe**", "**luxury brand**", "**upper-range brand**" and "**brand**", the above approaches tend to dichotomicly distinguish between luxury brands and non-luxury brands (de Barnier/ Rodina/Vallette-Florence, 2006), thereby taking a quite simplistic view on the concept of the brand. In order to adopt a more differentiated perspective, in this thesis, Heine's definition of the luxury brand will thus be complemented by Kapferer's four-stage brand pyramid.

In light of the above, it appears especially important to demarcate the luxury brand from the "upper-range" or **premium brand** (Kapferer, 2012, p. 66). That is to say, unlike luxury brands, premium brands cannot lose sight of the "value-for-money ratio" and therefore primarily focus on their functional features (Heine, 2011, p. 53). Also, compared to luxury brands, premium brands emphasise to a lesser extent the notions of heritage, storytelling and customer relationship management (Kapferer/Bastien, 2009, p. 315ff.).

In further remarks, Kapferer (2012, p. 67) differentiates between the idea of luxury and that of **fashion**, asserting that luxury would run diametrically contrary to fashion in that "luxury is enduring" owing to its worship of such explicitly timeless values as history, tradition and heritage whereas fashion "is obsessed with being out of fashion" and hence innately "ephemeral". With reference to the much-quoted McKinsey report (1990) that identified 35 product categories within the luxury industry among whose the most cited are fashion, cars, leather goods, perfumes, shoes, watches, jewellery and spirits (The Economist, 1993, p. 91), this distinction, however, will not be adhered to. Instead of opposing luxury and fashion on equal conceptual terms, one can rather assume a kind of hierarchy between both ideas. Luxury can thus be understood as overarching industry in which fashion represents one possible product subcategory. Yet, as the fashion territory is not confined to luxury but is also exploited in sectors being fundamentally different from that of luxury[7], only those fashion brands will be considered in this thesis that are first and foremost categorised as luxury brands in line with Heine's definition as provided above[8].

---

7 For instance, the mass retailer *H&M* is referred to as "big player in 'fast-fashion'" (Siegle, 2012).

8 In earlier works, Kapferer/Bastien (2009, p. 315) seem to follow the author's rationale and say that as regards the link between luxury and fashion, "success relies on a tandem arrangement, where you have a brand (which covers the luxury side) and a creator (who covers the fashion side)".

1.3 Functions and effects of the luxury brand on the consumer

Brands offer different functions to the consumer. From a behavioural perspective, they provide general guidance, increase market transparency and reduce the consumer's research efforts by facilitating both the identification of labelled products and/or services and the subsequent purchase decision (orientation and information function). Also, the consumer can substantially decrease his transaction costs within the buying process and compensate for his unilateral information deficit thanks to the reputation that trusted brands have successfully established in the marketplace (safety and confidence-building function). Finally, brands may fulfil the consumer's desire for self-expression, recognition within his reference group and demarcation from members of lower social strata (prestige and image-forming function) (Burmann/ Meffert/Koers, 2005, p. 10ff.).

These functions also hold true for luxury brands. Yet, whereas generic and upper-range brands are meant to primarily perform the elementary orientation and safety functions, as to luxury brands, emphasis is put on the symbolic function (Lasslop, 2005, p. 475): "More than other products, luxury items are bought for what they mean, beyond [for] what they are" (Dubois/Paternault, 1995, p. 71). The main benefit of luxury brands is hence expressed in the opportunity to publicly demonstrate one's values, moral concepts and belonging to a particular social stratum (**demarcation function**) and to conspicuously communicate affluence and the attainment of a certain social position (**status function**) through the purchase and possession of luxury items (Meffert/Lasslop, 2004, p. 932). In line with the ultimate raison d'être of luxury that appears to be rooted rather in the possession of a luxury good than in the latter's consumption (Jäckel/Kochhan, 2000, p. 75), "luxury brands [accordingly] are to civilians the equivalent of what medals are for military officers. They are a personal reward, a deep pleasure and a message about where the person stands in the social hierarchy" (Kapferer, 2012, p. 66). Luxury brands thus generate major **non-functional benefits** that can be directed either **outwardly** (e.g. social prestige or self-distinction) or **inwardly** (e.g. self-actualisation or hedonic shopping experience) (Valtin, 2005, p. 10). In this connection, Leibenstein (1950, p. 188ff.) argues that both the demarcation and status functions of luxury brands would be reflected in the consumer's demand behaviour vis-à-vis these brands and distinguishes between the bandwagon, the snob and the Veblen effect. The **bandwagon effect** describes the extent to which the demand for a luxury brand augments as the number of people buying it increases and thus translates the consumer's desire for social conformity and acceptance within his reference group. The **snob effect** in contrast indicates the extent to which the demand for a luxury brand decreases as the number of people buying it increases and is hence an expression for the consumer's aspiration for clear demarcation and social elevation. The **Veblen effect** finally shows how the consumer's propensity to buy a luxury brand augments as the latter's price is raised. Here, the consumer aims at demonstrating material affluence and financial power in *order to impress his relevant social environment.*

2. Explanations on the notion of art

Whereas there seems to be a broad consensus within the scientific community on the idea that the perception of art substantially differs from the perception of other objects (Joy/Sherry, 2003), eventually turning the specific views on, and appreciations of art into a distinct field of inquiry (Berlyne, 1974; Funch, 1997), there is substantial disagreement about the concrete definition of the notion of art (Hagtvedt/Patrick, 2008, p. 380).

Although the ongoing philosophical debate on how to determine the essence of art clearly goes beyond the scope of this thesis, it is, however, necessary to specify this term in the particular context of LBACs. Instead of drawing up a definition that claims to fully grasp the elusive quality of art or to keep its absolute validity outside of this thesis, it will thus rather be about developing a kind of working definition that best suits the purposes of this thesis by allowing both differentiating the notion of LBACs from related concepts and empirically capturing the occurrence of art within the scope of luxury branding. To this end, hereinafter, the aim will hence be to provide a brief overview of selected perspectives on art, to discuss dominating approaches to the operationalisation of the abstract nature of art and to briefly present the different art forms that may be relevant in order to organise the manifold manifestations of LBACs into distinct types.

2.1 Different perspectives on art

With the objective of approximating as closely as possible the intangible concept of art, in the following, three different perspectives will be provisionally adopted and evaluated in terms of their practicability for the empirical purposes of this thesis.

(1) Etymological perspective on art: Etymologically, the word art derives from the Latin term 'ars', the latter being equivalent to the Greek word 'techne', and can be translated as skill, craft or craftsmanship. In this regard, the respective skill is considered as the result of technical learning, repeated practice and assiduous work (Parry, 2008). 'Artes', the plural of the word 'ars', thus refers to craftsmen's mechanical skills that are based on clearly specified systems of rules, which always need to be strictly observed, and aim at producing solely useful objects (Fuchs, 2011, p. 44). Taking the etymological meaning of art as a starting point for the discussion on its different possible interpretations, there is no distinction between the artist and the artisan. Rather, the notion of art is perceived as purely functional and only applies to those objects that unmistakably represent mainstays of human existence (Scott, 2010, p. 74; similar: Osborne/Sturgis/Turner, 2012, p. 15).

Yet, the etymological perspective on art has no longer much relevance today. While it is true that, in the Middle Ages, the artist was still primarily considered as artisan "covering the walls of churches, public buildings and the houses of the wealthy", with the artistic focus being put on the idealised expression and submissive promotion of religious truths (Shiner, 2003, p. 28ff.; similar: Koller, 2007, p. 114; Osborne/Sturgis/Turner, 2012, p. 30), the artist's social role radically changed in the wake of the transition to a civil society in the early Modern Age. By liberating himself from the medieval guild system, the artist became emancipated, discovered himself as a confident and self-determinedly acting subject, started to personally sign his artworks and began to create works whose ultimate purpose was no longer the artistic mediation of the Christian faith or the endorsement of a certain prince's power, but the subjective expression of his particular sensations and experiences in his living environment (Krieger, 2007, p. 16ff.).

As the notion of art has thus been distancing itself from its etymological roots over time (Ullrich, 2006, p. 189ff.), approaching the former via its original meaning does no longer correspond to the manifold and oftentimes also purposeless forms of creative expression that the arts may take on today. What can, however, be retained from the etymological perspective is that **art is usually produced by human beings through the technical arrangement of form, material and colour** (Osborne/Sturgis/Turner, 2012, p. 9).

Since taking the etymological perspective on art does not, due to its both outdated and too narrow understanding of the term, offer sufficiently valuable clues to the characteristics of those artefacts that are today commonly qualified as art, a more abstract and hence potentially more revealing perspective will subsequently be taken.

(2) Aesthetical-philosophical perspective on art: As a response to the etymological definition of art having become obsolete, various philosophers have subsequently tried to identify fundamental properties by which the universal essence of art could be captured and explained as an indispensable element of human culture, thereby establishing the discipline of aesthetics (Gethmann-Siefert, 1995, p. 17ff.). Originally deriving from the Greek word 'aisthesis', the term aesthetics can be translated as sensation or perception and was eventually coined by the German philosopher Alexander Gottlieb Baumgarten as a label for the study of artistic experience and sensual perception (Freeland, 2003, p. 23). The concepts of **art as beauty, hedonistic pleasure or a matter of taste** have long been key issues in this regard (Cothey, 1990, p. 152ff.; Gethmann-Siefert, 1995, p. 54ff.; Schmücker, 1998, p. 19). As the different aesthetical-philosophical perspectives on art are, though, as manifold as the number of philosophers having mused about this question, it would be beyond the scope of this thesis to provide a comprehensive discussion on these myriad positions[9]. Yet, such a synoptic overview can be considered as being superfluous anyhow since all attempts to conclusively ascertain the particular nature of art appear to have finally failed (Torres/Kamhi, 2000, p. 95) in times where a major part of art is no longer appealing nor beautiful, but oftentimes explicitly refuses to be described by such terms and deliberately uses forms of creative expression that can rather be referred to as displeasing, repugnant or even downright shocking (Figal, 2012, p. 70; Osborne/ Sturgis/Turner, 2012, p. 2).

The placelessness of art within the field of philosophy can eventually be ascribed to the concept's inherent sensuousness and **visual nature** on the one, and its futileness and **purposelessness**[10] on the other hand. While the former has led to the impossibility of fully comprehending the emotional value of art through language or the intellect, thereby effectively preventing the aesthetics from evolving into a discrete philosophical discipline (Schmücker, 1998, p. 33ff.), the latter has entailed the questioning of the importance of art for human action and culture (Gethmann-Siefert, 1995, p. 7).

Even if the discipline of aesthetics has successfully broadened the concept of art beyond its original meaning by regarding art as **embodied human expression that is not driven by any "contrived function"** or utility (Hagtvedt/Patrick, 2008, p. 380), it does not substantially contribute to a better understanding of the elusive nature of art.

9 For an overview of the different perspectives on art in aesthetics see e.g. Hauskeller (2000).

10 As one's behaviour is generally explained teleologically, that is, "by describing how it helps [...] to satisfy [...] [one's] wants and needs [...], all human behaviour [...] can ultimately be understood in terms of its survival value". Yet, providing that art has no end in itself, it does not contribute to any other aim. From the teleological perspective, the existence of art can thus be considered as being "anomalous" (Cothey, 1990, p. 1ff.). This self-referential philosophy, under which art neither has a social function nor can be categorised by subject matter, style or any other distinctive exterior feature, traces back to the French slogan 'L'art pour l'art' and was initially coined by the French philosopher Victor Cousin in the early 19th century (Osborne/Sturgis/Turner, 2012, p. 89).

As a result, it is finally explored to what extent the comparatively more tangible legal sciences can produce useful insights into the distinctive features of art.

(3) Legal perspective on art: As the freedom of art represents one of the human rights stipulated by the German Constitution, the concept of art accordingly constitutes a legal term that is granted constitutional protection (GG Art. 5(3)). In order to decide whether a given matter of fact can be considered as art and may thus fall within the scope of protection of the German Basic Law, it has consequently become necessary to define the abstract notion of art (Scholz, 2013, Art. 5(3) GG, para. 25).

Historically, the German Federal Constitutional Court draws a distinction between three complementary concepts of art that result from different, successive landmark decisions (Pieroth/Schlink, 2012, p. 159). While the **formal concept of art** provides that only those activities should be understood as art that can phenotypically be attributed to one of the traditional art forms (e.g. literature, painting, sculpture or theatre) (BVerfGE 67, 213/225), the **substantive concept of art** requires that an individual's free inventive creation materialises in a certain, physically perceptible use of forms (BVerfGE 30, 173/188). Pursuant to the comparatively more abstract **open concept of art**, in turn, the primary characteristic of artistic expression lies in the possibility, based on the continuous interpretation of the former's manifold connotations, to extract an ever more far-reaching meaning from this artistic expression, thereby giving rise to a virtually inexhaustible provision of information (BVerfGE 67, 213/226). Since the open concept of art best takes into account modern artistic principles such as **difficult-to-access inherent laws, autonomy, singularity and diversity**, it has eventually emerged as the prevailing legal definition of art (Scholz, 2013, Art. 5(3) GG, para. 22).

Adopting the legal perspective on art produces two essential benefits. First, while acknowledging that an absolute definition of art can possibly never be drawn up (Pieroth/Schlink, 2012, p. 159), it reinforces though the necessity to subsume the idea of art under a tangible category, thereby legitimately differentiating between art and non-art (Scholz, 2013, Art. 5(3), paras 25 and 39). Second, by simultaneously approaching the concept of art from different angles, it allows for the **heterogeneous forms of appearance** that art may take on today. Yet, the legal concept of art does not prove effective for the empirical purposes of this thesis: Since the open concept of art ultimately implies that all those activities are granted the status of art that can, in the broadest sense, be interpreted as such, it accordingly does not provide any concrete criterion for the decision on whether the collaborative behaviour by a given luxury brand must be classified as a LBAC or not.

2.2 Contemporary approaches to the operationalisation of art

The incapacity shown by the above perspectives on art to define essential attributes that would be unique to art or common to all empirically observable artistic manifestations led some scholars to assert that one will never find a convincing answer to the question on the concrete nature of art (e.g. Gaut, 2002, p. 140; Torres/Kamhi, 2000, p. 94ff.). As a remedy, it appears to have become a regular practice to approach the definition of art rather via the question **'Who decides on the status of art?'** (Matthews, 2002, p. 110) than via the attempt to identify any fundamental characteristics according to which art can be distinguished from other aesthetic or visual concepts (Irvine, 2013). To this end, it is necessary to first appoint an agent being outside of the concrete artefact or performance to whom one wants to concede the right to interpret this same artefact or performance as art, before art can effectively be distinguished from non-art. This procedure, which is usually grouped under the so-called "**open-ended theories**" (Torres/Kamhi, 2000, p. 95), will also be followed in this thesis. Hereinafter, two selected, dominating open-ended approaches to the operationalisation of art will be discussed and assessed with respect to their practicability for the empirical purposes of this thesis.

(1) Consumer-focused approach to art: One common strategy to avoid defining the concrete features of art is to leave the ultimate judgement to the individual art consumer and to argue that art is what the viewer categorises as such (Bourdieu/ Darbel, 1991, p. 37ff.; Dewey, 1958, p. 35ff.). The benefit of this definition lies in its all-embracing character: Anything might be qualified as art – provided that the viewer gives his consent. The weakness of this approach is, though, a direct result of the latter fact: Based on this definition, one will never reach an externally verifiable judgement on whether a certain artefact should be classified as artwork since the ultimate evaluation will always entirely depend on the particular viewer's appraisal – and might consequently substantially vary among different individuals. This downside is all the greater as this thesis is neither consumer- nor effect-oriented, but aims at empirically identifying, based on externally verifiable attributes, different types of LBACs. The consumer-focused approach to art accordingly does not prove convenient in this context and will thus not be adhered to.

(2) Institution-focused approach to art: Another strategy to prevent reflecting on the distinct nature of art represents the institutional perspective on art that assumes that art can only be recognised as such by reference to a certain social framework (Danto, 1964, p. 580). Here, the status as a work of art is something conferred upon artefacts by people acting on behalf of the art world[11], with the latter being an institution in the sense of an "established practice" (Dickie, 1974, p. 31ff.; similar: Dickie, 1984, p. 49ff.). Accordingly, "what makes something an artwork is not an observable property in an artwork itself. The work is [rather] a node in a network of forces without which it would be unrecognizable, literally invisible" (Irvine, 2013). Constituting today one of the most influential approaches to defining art (Stecker, 2002, p. 135; Cothey, 1990, p. 127), the institutional perspective offers two central benefits. First, just as the consumer-oriented approach, it features an all-encompassing quality that allows classifying virtually everything as a work of art on condition that a recognised authority within the art world indicates the latter as such. Second, in contrast to the consumer-oriented approach, the institutional definition of art distinguishes itself by its practical applicability. Once one has bindingly agreed on superordinate categories that make up the institutionalised art world, it is relatively easy to identify the individual institutions being authorised to grant the status of art and, based on these institutions' appraisal, to decide whether a given artefact can be categorised as an artwork or not. Given the need for a definition of art that can, due to its high levels of simplicity and manageability, be best operationalised in the context of LBACs, in the following, the institutional perspective on art will be adhered to under which

> Art is understood as a communicative act pursuant to which authorised institutions within the art world assign the status of art to a given artefact. Accordingly, an artefact is considered being art "if it is called art, written about in an art magazine, exhibited in a museum or bought by a private collector" (McEvilley, 1997).

McEvilley's appended quotation underlines the necessity to describe more specifically the bodies being involved in the above communicative act and to define in detail the groups of institutions that shall be entitled to grant the status of art in the scope of this thesis, thereby rendering the notion of art even more "operational" (Irvine, 2013). With reference to Luhmann's (1995, p. 215ff.) theory on the increased specialisation of the so-called "art system", a tripartite set of organisations and their respective judgement of a given artefact will subsequently be followed in order to decide whether the latter can be regarded as an artwork:

11 For an in-depth discussion on the concept of the "artworld" see e.g. Danto (1964).

1. Institutions:	State and national museums, (private) art associations, exhibition venues and cultural centres, art foundations, art academies, galleries, art fairs, non-commercial off-spaces as well as auction houses;
2. Individuals:	Museum directors, curators, art patrons and art donors, art collectors as well as art critics;
3. Media:	Periodicals and professional trade magazines, daily press (feuilletons) and others (e.g. fashion and lifestyle magazines).

In light of the limited scope of this thesis, detailed definitions of the above three groups and their respective constituent parts have to be omitted in favour of a mere enumeration, thereby banking on the reader's existing knowledge and good sense in the area of art and the latter's publicly accessible ecosystem (Filicko/Lafferty, 1999, p. 6).

Being qualified as generally accepted sources of recognition and critique (e.g. Freeland, 2003, p. 113ff.; Irvine, 2013; Morris, 1971, p. 68ff.), the above tripartition thus serves as a controllable, both quantitative and qualitative indicator for granting the status of art to a given artefact. In practical terms, this means that, when testing all existing luxury brands for potential collaborations with the arts, each time, it must be checked whether the detected object, product, practice, campaign, event, organisation or individual in question is mentioned, promoted, collected and/or exhibited by one of the above parties involved. Adhering to the institutional definition of art will hence not only both substantially facilitate and systematise the empirical research process, but will also ensure the integration of comparatively young and unorthodox art forms such as video or performance art for instance, which are commonly showcased in artist run off-spaces, promoted by eccentric curators and discussed by non elitist media[12] (cf. B.2.3 for a more detailed discussion on the different art forms).

After all, in order to deliver a consistent language use throughout this work and to assure a shared understanding of the deployed concepts, the following terminology is hereinafter referred to:

12 To give but one example, the German Interview Magazine featured a review of the collaboration between the Champagne brand *Dom Pérignon* and the video artist Leo Kuelbs (Stelzner, 2012) (for more information on this collaboration cf. footnote 39).

Art	Refers to the general overarching discipline of art.
Arts	Refer to the collectivity of the different art forms.
Artwork	Refers to a particular piece of art as final outcome of artistic activities.
Artist	Refers to a person engaged into the artistic creation of an artwork.
Art world	Refers to the collectivity of people being involved in the production, commission, preservation, promotion, criticism and/or sale of art.

2.3 Classification of the different art forms

While the institutional definition of art aims at distinguishing between art and non-art, it gives no indication of the possible forms of appearance that art may take on. Although it might seem contradictory at first sight to fill the originally open-ended idea of art with concrete types of artistic manifestation, general experience suggests that the institutions that are accorded the authority to grant the status of art usually refer to recurrent art forms, thereby effectively securing the acceptance of their authority by the public in the long run. For the sake of simplification and with a view to an enhanced understanding of the artistic genres, a tripartite classification is subsequently followed that differentiates between non-time-based, time-based and hybrid art forms (Frisk/Karlsson, 2011, p. 277)[13].

(1) Non-time-based art forms: Non-time-based art forms and their consumption by the art viewer are first and foremost characterised by their independence from the time criterion. This means that the artistic production of an artwork commonly precedes the latter's presentation to the public and is hence regularly separated in time from the actual art consumption process. As such, an artwork can be repeatedly exhibited, experienced and consumed, on each occasion in a virtually unchanged manner (Frisk/Karlsson, 2011, p. 277). The non-time-based art forms essentially comprise **literature** as well as the visual and conceptual arts. The **visual arts** create artworks that one can look at and that are thus both figurative and tangible in nature, thereby including artistic disciplines such as drawing, painting, sculpture, photography and filmmaking, but also encompassing the so-called applied arts (e.g. industrial, graphic and fashion design, architecture as well as the decorative arts) that can be distinguished by the application of artistic principles such as aesthetics or design to functional objects of everyday use (Esaak, 2011a). The **conceptual arts**, in turn, refer

13 Although the dichotomy applied by Frisk/Karlsson (2011, p. 277), who demarcate art forms being "contained in time" from those being "embedded in time", served as the main literature reference, in this thesis, an autonomous terminology is followed for the sake of an improved conceptual clarity.

to artworks in which the underlying idea takes precedence over traditional graphic principles and material concerns: "In conceptual art the idea or concept is the most important aspect of the work. When an artist uses a conceptual form of art, it means that all of the planning and decisions are made beforehand and the execution is a perfunctory affair. The idea becomes a machine that makes the art" (LeWitt, 1967, p. 79). Conceptual artworks, which are often materialised in some kind of physical installation, accordingly become solely comprehensible through the intellectual confrontation by the art viewer with the elementary thought that has initially motivated the artist to create these artworks (Kosuth/Holzer/Ueltzhoeffer, 2012).

(2) Time-based art forms: Time-based art forms and their experiencing by the art consumer, by contrast, distinguish themselves by their constitutive dependence on the time criterion; that is to say, they deliberately use time as a both formative and structuring artistic element. Time-based art forms are consequently characterised by having a clear beginning and ending in time and become manifest in ephemeral performances, short-lived happenings or participatory art making events. There is hence usually simultaneity between the creative art production process performed by the artist and the art consumption process undergone by the audience. Time-based art forms typically encompass the performing arts, performance art as well as the participatory arts – although the definitional boundaries between these concepts appear to be rather blurred (Green, 2011). In the **performing arts**, the artist deploys his own body, face, voice or simple physical presence as artistic medium. Therefore also being qualified as conceptual antithesis of the visual arts in which the artist uses tangible materials to create physically perceptible artworks, the performing artist refers to the spoken word, music, dance, opera, theatre, magic or the circus arts in order to convey his creative visions (Bhuyan, 2012). **Performance art**, in turn, corresponds to a comparatively more experimental form of live expression that aims at the clear demarcation from the performing arts by neither depending on conventional spatial settings such as theatres or concert halls nor serving any commercial purposes: "Artists saw (and see) the movement as a means of taking their art directly to a public forum, thus completely eliminating the need for galleries, agents, brokers, tax accountants and any other aspect of capitalism. It's a sort of social commentary on the purity of art" (Esaak, 2011b). The **participatory arts** finally refer to an interactive approach to artistic live expression under which the audience is directly involved into the art production process. Since this non-elitist artistic practice turns the formerly passive art viewer into an active co-creator being on par with the actual artist, participatory artworks remain incomplete and cannot reach their full artistic expression without the effective contribution by the art consumer (Goldenberg/Reed, 2008).

(3) Hybrid art forms: The emergence of new media[14] technologies and the concomitant on-demand access to digital content any time, anywhere and on any device (Dalloz, 2011) have brought about a third category of art. The so-called "hybrid art forms" combine elements of the non-time-based art forms with features of the time-based art forms through the convergence of "artistic and technological thinking" (Frisk/Karlsson, 2011, p. 277). While the hybrid art forms accordingly produce artworks that, by their very nature, can be compared to the creative outputs of the more traditional visual and performing arts (e.g. digital poetry, live painting or multimedia performances), their delivery to a commonly digitally connected and interactive audience is performed in real time with the aid of new media technologies (Freeland, 2003, p. 210). Consequently also referred to as "**new media arts**", the hybrid art forms comprise, amongst others, **digital art**, **video art** and **computer art** (Tribe/Jana, 2006). Since the conceptual boundaries between the latter are rather fuzzy and of little interest to the purposes of this thesis, they will not be further discussed here.

3. Explanations on Luxury Brand-Art Collaborations

After the theoretical foundations of the notion of the luxury brand and that of art have been laid, both ideas will now be merged together, thereby giving rise to the composite concept of Luxury Brand-Art Collaborations (LBACs). Hereafter, the goal will be to provide a brief overview on the latter's history, to discuss existing literature concepts that deal with these interdisciplinary relationships and to develop an autonomous definition on the basis of which related concepts are finally demarcated.

3.1 History

The large number of LBACs, which one can currently observe in the international luxury goods industry (Boche, 2010), may be partly ascribed to the "**structural proximity** that luxury brands have always had with art" (Kapferer/Bastien, 2012, p. 107). Many authors across the international luxury brand management literature accordingly underline the **historic link between both ideas** (see, amongst others, Chevalier/Mazzalovo, 2012, p. 208ff.; Kapferer/Bastien, 2012, p. 32ff.; Tungate, 2009, p. 105ff.). Yet, they usually only address the conceptional interdependence between the abstract notion of luxury and that of art[15], while refraining from retracing the precise origins of the deliberate, publicly visible collaborations that luxury brands and the arts have been time and again entering in recent years. In order to reproduce the

14 As regards the new media phenomenon see e.g. Feldman (1997) or Flew (2005).

15 For an in depth-discussion on the conceptual demarcation between the notion of luxury and that of art see e.g. Kapferer/Bastien (2012, p. 32ff.).

beginnings of the latter's "**current love affair**" (Michau, 2009), subsequently, especially press articles are therefore referred to since they commonly put a special focus on describing the concrete evolutionary history of LBACs.

One of the first documented collaborations between a luxury (fashion) brand and the arts dates back to the 1920s when the Italian **fashion designer Elsa Schiaparelli teamed up with the Surrealist painters Salvador Dalí and Jean Cocteau** in order to generate new creative ideas for her clothing designs (Povoledo, 2012). In this context, Dalí is said to have literally created jewellery and dresses for Schiaparelli (Flamini, 2008). Likewise, in the 1930s, the Italian shoe manufacturer *Ferragamo* drew on Futurist painter Lucio Venna's distinct sense of aesthetics when producing the artworks for the brand's then advertising campaign, while Gianni Versace ordered inventive creations from artists such as Alighiero Boetti and Roy Lichtenstein to complement the launch of his collection (Proctor, 2009). Later on in the 1960s, the French couturier Yves Saint Laurent took not only inspiration from the painters Piet Mondrian and Pablo Picasso when developing the cutting patterns for his upcoming haute couture collection, but even printed Mondrian's famous multi-coloured rectangles onto his dresses (Maxwell, 2011).

An **important turning point** as to the different **collaborative patterns** between luxury brands and the arts could be observed in the 1980s when Alain Dominique Perrin, then president of the French high-end jeweller *Cartier*, created the contemporary **art museum** Foundation Cartier in Paris (Chevalier/Mazzalovo, 2012, p. 211). In the wake of the move from rather temporary one-off associations with isolated artists to a sustained long-term support of the contemporary artistic mindset, henceforward, luxury brands have been discovering both **more heterogeneous and versatile forms of LBACs**: "There has been a veritable fiesta of new creative collaborations, exploring fresh avenues for synergies and business development between the art world and the luxury industry" (Proctor, 2009).

The "**current art-luxe wave**" (Maxwell, 2011), however, can be considered as a relatively young phenomenon that has only been triggered in 1997 when **Marc Jacobs** was appointed artistic director at the French fashion house ***Louis Vuitton*** and initiated, within a very short period of time, several **high-profile collaborations with emerging pop and street artists**. In this regard, the American Jacobs successively commissioned graffiti artist Stephen Sprouse, pop art artist Takashi Murakami and appropriation artist Richard Prince to reinterpret the brand's iconic logo (Binlot, 2012). The pictures in figure 1 show three selected handbags from the limited edition collections that were designed, respectively, by Sprouse in 2001, Murakami in 2004 and Prince in 2007 for *Louis Vuitton.*

Having met a huge commercial success, *Louis Vuitton*'s highly mediatised artist co-operations are not only commonly referred to as **best practice example** that other luxury brands have since then been following (Boche, 2010; Chevalier/Mazzalovo, 2012, p. 210; Klanten/Ehmann/Sinofzik, 2012, p. 9; Maxwell, 2011; Michau, 2009), but also mark a **turning point as to the nature of art** that luxury brands request henceforth inspiration and value of. While luxury brands had formerly mainly been associated with rather traditional representations of art and strictly aesthetically oriented artists, today luxury brands also seek proximity with more **experimental types of artistic expression and eccentric artists** (Maxwell, 2011; Michau, 2009) who even use "rubbish" (instead of high-quality materials) in order to convey their creative visions (Kapferer/Bastien, 2012, p. 34).

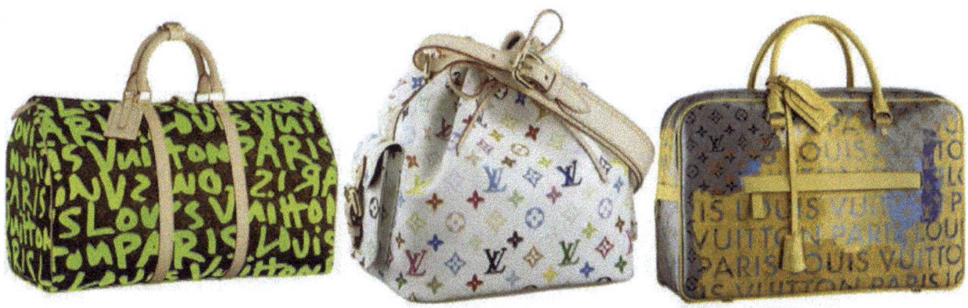

Sprouse Murakami Prince

Figure 1: Selected items from the limited edition collections designed by Sprouse, Murakami and Prince for *Louis Vuitton* (Source: Louis Vuitton Germany, 2013).

3.2 Existing literature concepts

Despite the strong, historically documented link between luxury brands and the arts, the international luxury brand management literature lacks clear, explicit and universally valid definitions of the concept of LBACs. Existing approaches are commonly limited to the emphasis on the general importance of these co-operations to the management of modern luxury brands (Chevalier/Mazzalovo, 2012, p. 211; Kapferer/Bastien, 2012, p. 34) and the maintenance of exclusivity (Catry, 2003, p. 13; Radon, 2012, p. 108ff.) or focus on selected aspects as regards their strategic and/or operational conception (Tungate 2009, p. 109). They refrain, though, from drawing up an overarching definition that would encompass the collectivity of these hetero-geneous, empirically observable cross-over partnerships. Also, existent terminology omits to define the notion of art and what exactly should be understood under this term within the scope of luxury branding. The absence of an unambiguous language use can here partially be ascribed to the fact that until now no comprehensive, empirically based typology of LBACs has been performed that would have required the development of such an all-embracing definition in the first place. Nonetheless, in the following, a selection of existing literature concepts of LBACs will be briefly discussed for the sake of completeness and in order to prepare the ground for deriving an independent definition of LBACs in the further course of this chapter.

The French brand strategist **Boche** (2010) refers to the mix between luxury brands and the arts by the term “Artketing” and highlights the heterogeneous approaches by which luxury brands incorporate art within their communication activities. In this regard, the author distinguishes art-related collaborations at the corporate level (e.g. art foundations, cultural patronage or sponsored exhibitions) from those at the brand respectively product level (e.g. co-created products in the form of limited editions). Irrespective of their concrete physical manifestation, these co-operations would permit luxury brands to “reconnect with their time” and to continually recreate the idea of “newness”. As a result, LBACs would give rise to a set of strategic issues such as an increased visibility in the marketplace, an improved likeability and a substantial gain in brand value.

Chevalier/Mazzalovo (2012, p. 209), in turn, assume that luxury brands decide to team up with the arts for quite opportunistic reasons since “having a strong cultural dimension can never have an adverse effect on a brand’s identity”. The authors accordingly qualify the concept of LBACs as a relatively straightforward approach which would consist of “associations between brands and art [where] designers and communicators in the luxury field have [...] recourse to artworks, either to compensate for their own wavering inspiration or simply to pay homage to the artist”. Luxury brands would consequently seek proximity to the arts in order to either innovate or advertise their product range.

Kapferer/Bastien (2012, p. 78), by contrast, remain rather abstract in their definition of LBACs by considering the latter as “symbiotic relationships” meant to bestow upon luxury brands the title of “patrons of emerging trends”. Here, joining forces with the arts would transform “luxury-brand objects” themselves into “works of contemporary art” whose goal would be to promote exquisite taste and to sustain the luxury brands’ claim to being bold and influential opinion leaders. Yet, the authors do not give further insights into the concrete associative mechanism that would turn luxury items into genuine artworks. Also, they limit their definition to collaborations between luxury brands and the so-called "non-popular arts", thereby excluding the possibility that luxury brands may also associate themselves with more traditional or even popular forms of artistic expression.

Maxwell (2011), Insight Director at the British design consultancy Pearlfisher, mainly focuses on the artist's role within LBACs and the latter's strategic benefit to luxury brands' endeavour to remain topical and prospect new clients. To that effect, LBACs are here defined as bilateral projects "where a brand commissions an artist to design, illustrate or do something inventive with a product" in order to "inspire delight" and inject "fresh talent into timeless craftsmanship". In this way, LBACs would permit luxury brands to "rekindle desire for a new generation of luxury followers". Yet, by confining her analysis exclusively to jointly created limited editions, Maxwell ignores the wide range of manifestations that LBACs empirically take on. Also, she restricts the different forms of integration of art into the luxury brand's universe to interventions by artists, thereby neglecting that luxury brands may also choose to link themselves to isolated artworks or entire art institutions.

The art journalist **Swengley** (2011) eventually sets restrictions as to the relevant product category and asserts that especially luxury fashion brands would initiate collaborations with the arts. These interdisciplinary relationships, which the author also treats as "crossovers", would primarily serve as a strategic brand-building tool that helps essentially old brands "to stay current, project a message and engage an audience".

3.3 Definition and conceptual demarcation

The above concepts of LBACs show two significant downsides. First, virtually all of them limit their examination to a few selected partnering opportunities, thereby leading one to assume that the mentioned options would represent the totality of the different possible forms of collaboration that luxury brands and the arts can choose to enter into with each other. Second, all of the above literature concepts tend to mix up approaches to definition on the one, and assumptions as to the nature of possible objectives that can be pursued by pooling resources with the arts on the other hand. Yet, the kind of objective potentially constitutes one of the attributes that will eventually allow the identification of different types of LBACs. Against this backdrop and with a view to the empirical purposes of this thesis, it therefore becomes necessary to draw up a definition under which all conceivable forms of LBACs can be grouped, without thereby already establishing any sort of predefining typology. Accordingly, in the context of this thesis,

> Collaborations between luxury brands and the arts are understood as any kind of deliberate associations between a luxury brand and art within the scope of which a luxury brand intentionally connects itself with a representative of the contemporary art world (i.e. artist, artwork or art institution) and the latter brings in a sensually perceivable artistic contribution.

Two aspects of the above definition need to be explained in greater detail. First, the idea of "deliberate associations" entails that only those alliances between luxury brands and the arts will be considered in this study that have been formed on purpose between both parties. As a result, only contemporary artists are included into the concept of LBACs since deceased artists can no longer give their explicit consent to such co-operations. Second, the necessity for the representative of the contemporary art world to make a concrete artistic contribution to the collaboration results in excluding those luxury brands from this investigation that simply metaphorically refer to the notion of art. In other words, solely verbally addressing the arts without thereby giving any tangible expression to this reference is not sufficient in order to be qualified as a LBAC in the context of this study. These precisions are all the more important since the conceptual proximity between the notion of luxury and that of art has led to the excessive use of such words as "art" or "artwork"[16] in both the communication and commercialisation strategies of luxury brands. Hence, given that the arts represent the "market of the single work", notably one-of-a-kind luxury items are regularly referred to as unmatched pieces of art (Kapferer/Bastien, 2012, p. 108). The definition of LBACs as laid down above expressly rejects these abstract references to art by luxury brands.

In order to develop a better understanding of the notion of LBACs, in the following, the latter is demarcated from related branding and marketing communication concepts.

(1) Celebrity endorsement: Using well-known and publicly admired people in order to promote one's product or brand is referred to as celebrity endorsement (Kamins, 1990, p. 4). Linking a brand to a famous person is here meant to draw additional attention to that brand and to shape the latter's positioning in the consumers' minds "by virtue of the inferences that consumers make based on their knowledge of the

16 The British manufacturer of high-end furniture *Silverlining*, for instance, uses the slogan "The Art of Furniture" (Silverlining, 2013) without, however, concretely collaborating with the arts in the proper sense of the word. Likewise, the *Staatliche Porzellan-Manufaktur Meissen* advertises its limited edition collections as "artworks", although the latter's creation usually does not involve any contribution by a representative of the contemporary art world as defined above (Meissen, 2013).

person" (Keller/Apéria/Georgson, 2012, p. 363). Even though some authors still assert that the use of celebrities would be incompatible with the essence of luxury brands (Kapferer/Bastien, 2012, p. 77), teaming up with prominent actors, pop singers, athletes or politicians enjoys today great popularity in the marketing practice of luxury brands[17] (Okonkwo, 2007, p. 156ff.).

Although both the concept of celebrity endorsement and that of LBACs are based on the association of a luxury brand with an additional symbol of communication, they differ in two fundamental respects. First, they are different with regard to the nature of the chosen reference object. Whereas celebrities form part of the global entertainment industry and are thus commonly known to a broad public (Friedman/Termini/Washington, 1976, p. 22), the art world constitutes a comparatively closed, if not elitist system that is generally not readily accessible for the average consumer (Chayka, 2012; Lee, 2012, p. 21; Saatchi, 2011). Second, whereas the reference to celebrities is usually one-directional by publicly leveraging the latter's outer attractiveness and worldwide fame in order to reinforce the promotional activities for an existing product or brand (Friedman/Friedman, 1979, p. 63), the transfer of associations, qualities and skills in the context of LBACs can also be bidirectional: The luxury brand either integrates art within its proprietary commercial universe or enters itself the art world (cf. "Direction of collaboration" in C.2.2.3).

It could eventually be objected that the above demarcation becomes meaningless if one assumes that celebrities, because of their predominantly creative professions as actors or singers, can be equated with artists and must hence be included into the concept of LBACs. Yet, according to the institutional definition of art, the idea of the celebrity can relatively clearly be distinguished from that of the artist as the former is commonly not acknowledged by the institutions to which was ascribed the authority to grant the status of artist to a given person. The institutional approach to art thus avoids entering the highly ideological debate on the artistic quality of the performance delivered by a celebrity-actor or -singer as opposed to that delivered by a 'genuine' artist (Nehb, 2013) respectively on the difference between "serious" and "entertaining" music (Hagestedt, 2008).

(2) Creative director: The creative director[18] of a luxury goods company is understood as an internal brand ambassador whose main task is not only to identify,

17 The endorsement of the French luxury brand *Louis Vuitton* by prominent persons such as Mikhail Gorbachev or Andre Agassi serves here as an illustrative example (Tungate, 2009, p. 141).

18 In the case of a (luxury) fashion brand, the function of the creative director is often also referred to as "fashion designer" (Bruce/Kratz, 2007, p. 137; Topping, 2012).

shape and translate upcoming trends into the creation of avant-garde product lines, but also to represent the brand to the outside by providing the latter with "a recognisable face that both fronts and reflects the label" (Topping, 2012). As a result, high-profile fashion designers like Marc Jacobs for *Louis Vuitton* or Karl Lagerfeld for *Chanel* usually maintain a permanent relationship with the luxury brand and play a pivotal role in defining the latter's commercial strategy in the long term[19] (Amed, 2013; Bruce/Kratz, 2007, p. 137ff.; Kapferer, 2006, p. 73; Okonkwo, 2007, p. 165).

Even if one might be tempted to include the creative director into the concept of LBACs due to his direct contribution to the luxury brand's "artistic inventiveness" (Kapferer, 2012, p. 70; similar: Chevalier/Mazzalovo, 2012, p. 209; Karpik, 2011, p. 201; The Observer, 2003) and propensity to stage himself as an eccentric artist (Pantazi, 2013), in this thesis, he is regarded as constituent and thus indissociable part of the luxury brand's distinctive universe[20] (Bruce/Kratz, 2007, p. 137ff.). As such, he is not a representative of the art world as provided in the above definition of LBACs, but simply renders the luxury brand's regular commercial offering possible (Amed, 2013; Kapferer/Bastien, 2012, p. 37).

(3) Co-branding: "Co-branding – also called brand bundling or brand alliances – occurs when two or more existing brands are combined into a joint product or marketed together in some fashion" (Keller, 1998, p. 283). Co-brandings have lately become a popular practice also in the field of luxury brand management since they enable luxury brands to quite easily tap into new customer segments, to enlarge their scope by embracing new technologies, to increase their geographic reach, to rejuvenate their image or to broaden their product range (Regier/Bulut, 2012, p. 41ff.; similar: Keller/Apéria/Georgson, 2012, p. 343). Like LBACs, co-brandings involve the linking of a (luxury) brand to an additional image object in order to further enhance, enrich or modify the brand's current positioning (Baumgarth, 2008, p. 194). Yet, whereas the concept of LBACs builds on the integration of an artistic contribution that, by its very nature, is "devoid of any rational [that is for-profit] function" (Kapferer/Bastien, 2012, p. 37), co-brandings are characterised by the association of two (or more) purely commercially oriented brands (Levin/Davis/Levin, 1996, p. 296). While the scope of co-brandings is therefore usually limited to the habitual environment of the involved brands (i.e. the marketing world), the interdisciplinary

---

19 Against this backdrop, it is hardly surprising that, in June 2013, the shares of the British fashion house *Mulberry* dropped by as much as eight percent immediately following the announcement by the brand's creative director Emma Hill to quit (Neville/Cochrane, 2013).

20 The brand universe "comprises the total brand and everything associated with it": From products and communication over brand values and brand personality to consumers (Braun, 1997, p. 116).

concept of LBACs is composed of two heterogeneous partners that move back and forth between commercial and artistic spheres (Klanten/Ehmann/Sinofzik, 2012, p. 9).

(4) Cause-related marketing: Cause-related marketing (CRM) is defined as "the process of formulating and implementing marketing activities that are characterized by an offer from the firm to contribute a specified amount to a designated cause when customers engage in revenue-providing exchanges that satisfy organizational and individual objectives" (Varadarajan/Menon, 1988, p. 60). Since the sponsoring of an art museum or the awarding of an art prize, which constitute today popular practices in the context of luxury branding and are covered by the above definition of LBACs, may be misleadingly qualified as cause-related, with the supported art institution or artist being the cause, demarcating the notion of LBACs from that of CRM appears indispensable. Both concepts differ in three main respects. First, while CRM always entails a tripartite structure (i.e. brand, cause agent and consumer; Vanhamme et al., 2012, p. 262), LBACs commonly translate into bipartite projects (i.e. luxury brand and art). Second, while the concept of CRM also comprises the endorsement of causes that have nothing to do with the arts, LBACs, by their very definition, necessarily always involve art in some fashion. Third, whereas the direct aid provided by the brand is usually exclusively financial in the case of CRM (Varadarajan/Menon, 1988, p. 59), LBACs boil down, if at all, to different forms of support of the art world (e.g. funds, know-how in branding and agenda setting, access to a valuable network or enhanced levels of awareness and public attention).

C. Attributes of Luxury Brand-Art Collaborations

1. Preliminary methodological remarks

Before the attributes of LBACs can be addressed, it is necessary to provide the methodological framework and to introduce the chosen research design under which these attributes will be systematically derived. Hereinafter, it is thus the aim to describe the concept of taxonomy as the underlying scientific rationale, to clarify the structural properties of attributes and to discuss different approaches to the latter's derivation.

1.1 Taxonomy: Classification vs. typology

In social sciences, the theory of taxonomy[21] is understood as the overarching discipline of both the classification and typology (Friedrichs, 1990, p. 90). Taxonomic analyses aim at a **simplified representation of reality by systematically organising a complex field of (empirical) entities** into groups, classes or types on the basis of these entities' structural similarities (Kluge, 1999, p. 43ff.; Sodeur, 1974, p. 9). Accordingly, "by maximizing both within-group homogeneity and between-group heterogeneity", the ultimate goal is to form "groups that are as distinct (non-overlapping) as possible, with all members within a group being as alike as possible" (Bailey, 1994, p. 1). Taxonomic considerations are thus meant to produce structures that show a medium degree of abstraction, thereby avoiding the extreme practices of individuation (strict consideration of each individual entity) and generalisation (derivation of conclusions supposed to be valid for all entities in a given field) (Knoblich, 1972, p. 142). Figure 2 illustrates how the taxonomy, as a function of the degree of abstraction, relates to the concepts of individuation and generalisation.

Taking into account the dichotomy applied by Baumgarth (2003, p. 46ff.), within the discipline of taxonomy, one can differentiate between two approaches of grouping entities by similarity, namely the classification and the typology[22]. The **classificatory**

21 As regards the concept of taxonomy see e.g. Sodeur (1974, p. 10).

22 Within the scientific community, there is, though, substantial disagreement on this demarcation. Pursuant to Bailey (1994, p. 6), the notions of taxonomy and classification can be used interchangeably, while the concepts of taxonomy and typology need to be strictly distinguished from one another. That is to say, whereas the typology is here understood as purely conceptual, the taxonomy is deemed to be solely empirical. According to Knoblich (1972, p. 142), however, a classification is performed by means of one single attribute and the latter's different characteristic values whereas a typology is performed by means of several attributes simultaneously. Sodeur (1974, p. 10), in contrast, qualifies the typology as the superordinate concept under which the classification represents one particular form. Friedrichs

approach is characterised by a **strict assignment of the analysed entities to given classes** and has to comply with the following three criteria (Friedrichs, 1990, p. 88ff.):

- Unambiguousness;
- Exclusivity;
- Completeness.

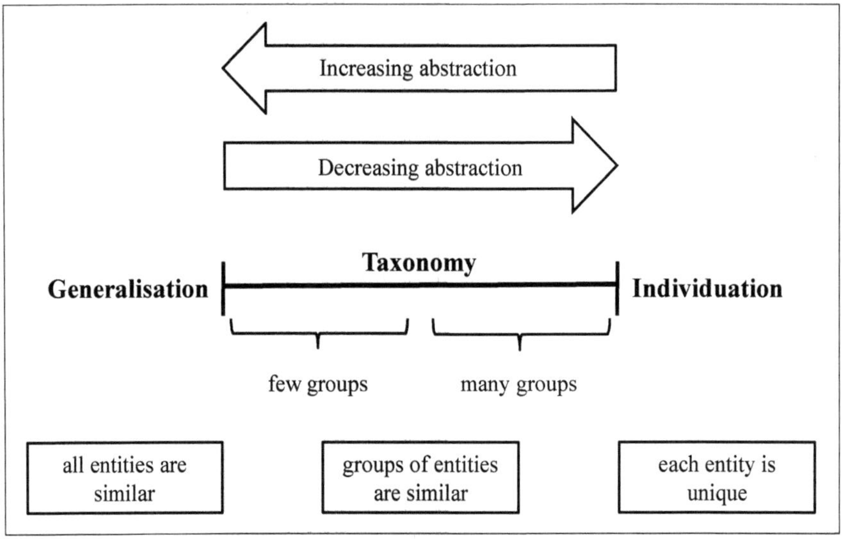

Figure 2: Theoretical classification of the taxonomy
(Source: Own representation based on Baumgarth, 2003, p. 46).

Unambiguousness is deemed to exist if each entity within a given field can be assigned the characteristic value of an attribute. Exclusivity occurs if only one single characteristic value applies to an entity. The criterion of completeness is met if each entity shows a characteristic value for each attribute. The constituent entities of one class consequently show exactly the same characteristic values for all attributes.

The **typological approach**, in contrast, is characterised by a comparatively **high degree of fuzziness** when it comes to assigning empirical entities to groups (Friedrichs, 1990, p. 89ff.; Tietz, 1960, p. 18ff.). This ambiguousness is essentially due to the simultaneous use of several attributes that a typology necessarily entails

(1990, p. 87ff.) and Kluge (1999, 32ff.), in turn, regard the classification and the typology as two coexisting approaches to the systematisation of complex fields of (empirical) entities.

(Knoblich, 1972, p. 142). The multiplicity of attributes accordingly prevents the researcher from clearly deciding whether one single attribute is both necessary and sufficient to structure a given field of entities (Friedrichs, 1990, p. 89). Also, under the typological approach, the entities must neither show characteristic values for all of the attributes nor conform to the criterion of exclusivity that must be observed under the classificatory approach (Baumgarth, 2003, p. 47).

Taxonomic considerations allow a choice between different approaches (Knoblich, 1972, p. 144ff.; Kolb, 1988, p. 41; Tietz, 1960, p. 14ff.):

- The heuristic or the empirical approach;
- The progressive or the retrograde approach.

The combination of several attributes for the purposes of forming different types can be based on either purely theoretical considerations or the empirical distribution of the analysed entities in reality. The former method, which is also referred to as **heuristic or artificial typology**, entails the hypothetical creation of ideal types whereas the latter method, which is also referred to as **empirical or natural typology**, involves the experiential formation of real types (Kluge, 1999, p. 58ff.).

The **progressive approach** regularly starts from the combination of separate attributes into different types that can subsequently be empirically tested for their actual existence and practical usefulness. Those types that cannot be observed in reality are congruously eliminated. Because of its gradual composition, the progressive method can also be referred to as synthetical approach. The conjunction of attributes can here result from either combinational logic (pursuant to the heuristic approach) or the description of real cases based on these attributes and the subsequent verification of similarities within the established groups (pursuant to the empirical approach). The **retrograde approach**, in contrast, sets in with empirical observations. Accordingly, the researcher is supposed to have a more or less concrete idea of real cases. The aim is here to identify those combinations of attributes that best demarcate the already known classes respectively types from one another. This method can therefore also be referred to as analytical approach (Knoblich, 1972, p. 144ff.).

1.2 Properties of attributes

Since taxonomic considerations that claim to be relevant from both a theoretical and empirical perspective are first and foremost dependent on the selection of meaningful attributes, the latter's structural properties will hereinafter be briefly explained. Attributes may vary in the following respects (Baumgarth, 2003, p. 48):

- Level of measurement;
- Possible characteristic values;
- Independence of the researcher;
- Significance;
- Exclusivity.

(1) Level of measurement: At the level of measurement, the researcher can choose among nominal, ordinal and metric attributes[23]. Nominal attributes allow distinguishing between entities depending on whether the latter show or do not show certain characteristic values. In other words, nominal attributes solely 'name' the different characteristic values that can be assigned to given entities, without thereby establishing any hierarchical order among the latter[24]. Ordinal attributes, in contrast, permit to determine a hierarchical order among these entities depending on the extent to which the latter possess a particular trait. Yet, one cannot make any statement about the concrete distance between the different characteristic values of an attribute. Metric attributes, in turn, enable the researcher not only to hierarchically rank the entities in question, but also to determine the size of the intervals between the different characteristic values (Baumgarth, 2003, p. 48ff.).

(2) Possible characteristic values: One can furthermore distinguish between alternative as against graded attributes. The alternative or exclusive attributes solely offer extreme characteristic values[25], thereby reflecting the underlying rationale of dichotomous traits. In the case of graded attributes, in contrast, a set of characteristic values connects both extreme cases. Graded attributes are therefore often expressed in ordinal measurement (Knoblich, 1972, p. 144; Kolb, 1988, p. 39).

---

23 Sodeur (1974, p. 40ff.) classifies both the nominal and ordinal attributes under the group of the qualitative attributes while referring to the metric attributes as quantitative attributes. With reference to Baumgarth (2003, p. 48), this classification is, however, not adhered to in this thesis since the conceptual duality of "qualitative" as against "quantitative" seems to be interpreted differently depending on the respective author (e.g. Knoblich, 1972, p. 143ff.; Kolb, 1988, p. 39).

24 The nature of nominal attributes is illustrated by the example of jersey numbers in basketball: A player featuring the number 30 is neither superior nor inferior to a player featuring the number 15.

25 In this thesis, the affiliation to a luxury conglomerate can be referred to as an alternative attribute since it only allows for the characteristic values 'yes' or 'no' (cf. "Affiliation" in C.2.2.1).

(3) Independence of the researcher: The independence of the researcher refers to the distinction between subjective and objective attributes. In the case of subjective attributes, the assignment of an entity to a specific characteristic value may turn out differently depending on the individual researcher's appraisal[26]. Objective attributes on the other hand are characterised by generally binding assignment rules and thus remain largely protected from potentially biased results (Knoblich, 1972, p. 144).

(4) Significance: Attributes may be further differentiated based on their importance to the formation of distinct types. Their varying weight within the research process permits here to produce a ranked order, where one discriminates between primary and secondary respectively constituent and accessory attributes. This approach to systematisation is, however, not deemed to be universally valid, but rather substantially differs according to the chosen research design and given field of investigation (Knoblich, 1972, p. 144).

(5) Exclusivity: Closely linked to the distinction pursuant to the relative significance of the attributes to the taxonomic study, a last differentiation can be made upon the degree of exclusivity that these attributes show. One accordingly distinguishes between monothetic as against polythetic attributes. Attributes that are both necessary and sufficient in order to decide on the assignment of an entity to a given class or type are referred to as monothetic attributes. Attributes, in contrast, that are neither necessary nor sufficient in order to decide on the affiliation of an entity to a given class or type are called polythetic attributes (Kluge, 1999, p. 78; Sodeur, 1974, p. 17ff.).

1.3 Alternative approaches to the selection of attributes

Attributes required for taxonomic considerations can be generated in two different ways: They can be derived either deductively or inductively (Heit, 2007, p. 2; Meidl, 2009, p. 18; Rips, 2001, p. 129). Deductive logic relates to a way of thinking that moves **from the more general to the more specific** and is also referred to as "**top-down**" approach (Trochim, 2006). **Deductive reasoning** can thus be defined as "drawing a conclusion that follows with logical necessity from given premises" (Oberauer et al., 2005, p. 1225). Solutions to current research questions are here rationally inferred from existing theories in relevant fields of inquiry (Wellhöfer, 1984,

26 In this thesis, the level of fit between the luxury brand and the arts can be considered as a comparatively subjective attribute given that the appraisal of whether there is a thematic coherence between both elements depends, at least partially, on the researcher's subjective perception of both the luxury brand's image and the nature of the collaborating arts.

p. 5) by combining given premises into novel scientific insights (Popper, 1971, p. 7ff.). Transferred to the context of this thesis, the deductive approach to knowledge discovery implies that possible attributes of LBACs are derived from existing taxonomic investigations in related fields of study and adapted in their characteristic values to the particularities of LBACs.

Inductive logic, in turn, derives **broader theoretical generalisations from specific empirical observations** and is also referred to as "**bottom up**" approach (Trochim, 2006). **Inductive reasoning** can hence be defined as "the process of inferring a general law or principle from the observation of particular instances" (Vickers, 2013). Transferred to the context of this thesis, the inductive approach to knowledge discovery implies the attempt to detect recurrent patterns or regularities of LBACs by analysing selected case studies. Based on these observations, one may develop tentative hypotheses about potentially useful attributes that can then be further explored and tested for their practical relevance by verifying whether these attributes also prove beneficial for describing similar empirical cases of LBACs.

The above approaches differ in three main respects. First, much greater importance is attached to the individual researcher in inductive than in deductive reasoning since the inductive method requires a high degree of independent, both abstract and creative thinking that prevents the researcher from losing himself in the arbitrary contingencies of the particular case. The demands on the responsible researcher to critically reflect his empirical discoveries and to persistently question whether his conclusions conform to scientific standards are all the greater as inductive reasoning occurs to a large extent via mental leaps, flashes of genius and sudden inspirations (Holl, 1999, p. 174). Secondly, whereas the deductive approach seems to be more appropriate if substantial research has already been undertaken in the given field of interest that may be referred to for the purposes of one's own investigation (Trochim, 2006), inductive reasoning "has the potential to be theoretically revealing" (Heit, 2007, p. 1) and may thus effectively explore comparatively ill-defined or highly complex research areas (Arthur, 1994, p. 406ff.). Thirdly, whereas the deductive technique allows deriving attributes without directly challenging the latter's empirical soundness, the inductive technique permits to make statements about the characteristics of empirically observable and hence real entities. Consequently, whereas insights that have been generated deductively possibly bear no relation to reality and are therefore also qualified as potentially dogmatic theories, findings that have been identified inductively are usually characterised by their strong practical pertinence and are accordingly also grouped under the positivist research paradigm (Wellhöfer, 1984, p. 5ff.; similar: Meidl, 2009, p. 112).

1.4 Description of the research design

With a view to systematising the various forms of LBACs, the utilisation of a **typology** – as opposed to a classification – seems to be more suitable for three main reasons. First, considering the current lack of empirical research in the field of LBACs, it appears more appropriate to leverage the exploratory nature of typologies (Aaker et al., 2011, p. 502), thereby aiming at producing first insights required for the subsequent formation of explicit scientific theories (Friedrichs, 1990, p. 89). Secondly, in light of the heterogeneous forms of appearance and the interdisciplinary composition of LBACs, it can be assumed that the **use of several attributes** will be necessary in order to fully grasp the variety of manifestations that LBACs can take on. Thirdly, since real, that is, empirically observable entities, among whom LBACs are to be counted, risk not complying with the strict criteria that need to be observed under the classificatory approach, a typological analysis is deemed to be more reasonable in the present case. Against this backdrop, the typology will follow the **empirical** (as against the heuristic) approach given the latter's higher correspondence to reality. Moreover, bearing in mind the current lack of tangible ideas about possible LBAC-types, the **progressive** (as against the retrograde) method will be adhered to. Altogether, one obtains hence a typological research design that is both empirical and progressive, and aims, based on a variety of attributes and a large number of **real cases**, at best reproducing the disparate field of LBACs in reality.

As regards the concrete process scheme, the following consecutive phases of investigation must be passed through before different types of LBACs can be identified (Baumgarth, 2003, p. 48 based on Knoblich, 1972, p. 143ff.):

1. **Selection of attributes of LBACs**;
2. **Empirical verification of selected attributes**;
3. **Derivation and description of different LBAC-types**.

While the second and third phase will be explained more in detail at the beginning of part D., hereinafter, a closer look will be taken at the selection of attributes of LBACs. Even if the above comparison of the deductive as against the inductive reasoning may indirectly suggest that one must necessarily opt for one of them (as if they represented mutually exclusive research approaches), both methods are commonly rather perceived as complementary and hence often represent sequenced phases within one and the same research process (Holl, 1999, p. 175; Trochim, 2006). The effectiveness of combining both methods appears to be even greater in the context of this thesis as the **unexplored character of LBACs** makes it necessary to approach the latter from different angles. In order to derive attributes that will eventually enable the empirical determination of different LBAC-types, a **dual approach to the selection of attributes of LBACs** will accordingly be followed.

Based on an **extensive literature review**, meaningful attributes of LBACs will first be derived deductively from related research areas and, if necessary, adapted in their characteristic values to the particularities of LBACs. Yet, since the latter's interdisciplinary nature goes beyond the fields of branding, marketing and business management, it can be assumed that the deductive approach will not produce the collectivity of attributes that are necessary to effectively describe LBACs in all their diversity. Hence, in addition to reviewing the relevant literature, **selected case studies** will be briefly analysed. In this regard, LBACs will be examined that formerly took place or are currently taking place in real life and whose specific manifestations allow deriving attributes that are particularly suitable for both describing and systematising LBACs. Deploying the exploratory case study method will thus permit to inductively derive attributes that would possibly not be included into the typological study if one exclusively relied upon evaluating the current state of research in adjacent disciplines (Schögel/Tomczak, 2009, p. 98).

Both the selection of the attributes and determination of the latter's characteristic values will be based on two criteria (Baumgarth, 2003, p. 56):

1. **Theoretical criterion**: Usefulness for the analysis and description of LBACs;
2. **Pragmatic criterion**: Easy measurability and verification of the attributes.

By leveraging the benefits of both the deductive and inductive reasoning within one and the same research design, the above methodology is likely to compile a comprehensive catalogue of attributes that will allow structuring at best the heterogeneous approaches to collaboration between luxury brands and the arts. The four-field matrix in figure 3 visually summarises the classification of the chosen study design into the different research options by highlighting in colour the approach being followed in this thesis.

2. Deductive attribute derivation

Prior to presenting the attributes that have been generated deductively, one necessarily needs to address the theoretical points of reference that have served as the initial starting point for detecting these attributes. Accordingly, those research areas that show significant thematic overlaps with the concept of LBACs will first be briefly discussed before the derived attributes will then be described in their specific characteristic values.

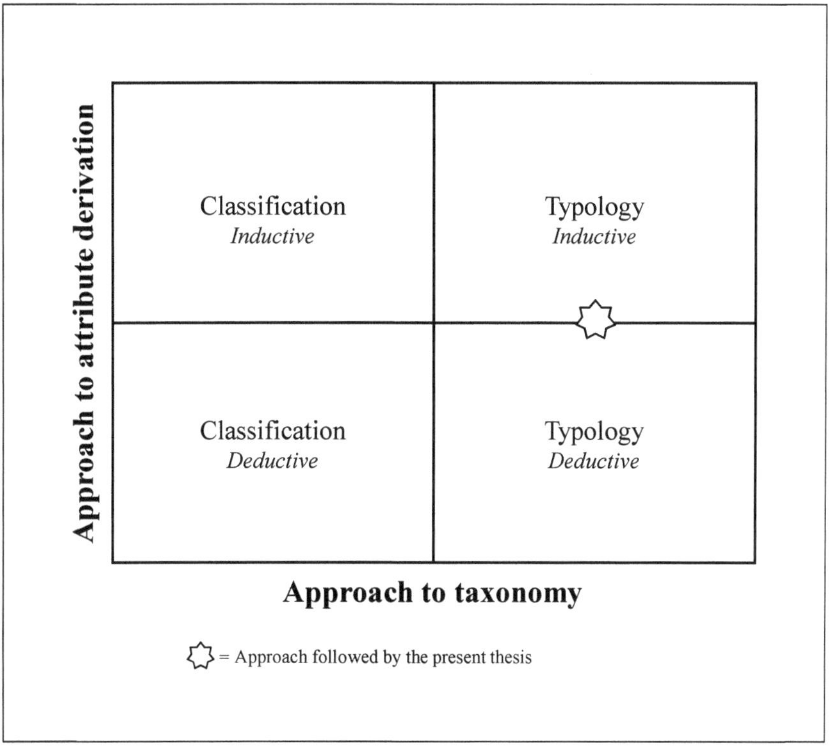

Figure 3: Chosen study design.

2.1 Theoretical points of reference

In the following, particular attention will be given to four distinct fields of inquiry that are, albeit to varying degrees, somehow related to the concept of LBACs: Namely the luxury brand management and brand leveraging literature on the one hand (that can also be summarised as brand-oriented research areas), and the interfirm co-operation and art-business management literature on the other hand (that can also be summarised as collaboration-oriented research areas). Subsequently, each discipline will be succinctly introduced, with special emphasis being placed on the conceptual link between the given field of inquiry and the notion of LBACs.

2.1.1 Luxury brand management

Irrespective of their actual pertinence, the famous "anti-laws of [luxury] marketing", which are persistently repeated by Kapferer/Bastien (2012, p. 65ff.), suggest that conventional principles of branding, communication and mass marketing cannot be directly transferred to the management of luxury brands. The latter's central issue would rather be about building up substantial barriers to consumption in order to protect the luxury brand's target clientele from undesired customers and to further enhance the luxury brand's symbolic value (Kapferer, 2012, p. 66ff.). Also referred to as "market shielding" (Meffert/Lasslop, 2004, p. 940), this strategy is usually implemented by charging a high price, following an exclusive distribution policy and putting particular emphasis on the brand's high-quality appeal (Lasslop, 2005, p. 477). Yet, luxury brands also need to reach high levels of awareness within the general public in order to effectively perform their social demarcation function and thus heavily rely on intensive media coverage (Kapferer, 2001, p. 358). The situation under which a luxury brand must be both known and coveted by the wide public while, however, being largely inaccessible for the average consumer is summarised by the apparently insoluble "paradox" of marketing luxury goods (Dubois/Paternault, 1995, p. 69). The need for a specifically designed marketing mix appears even more important in light of the distinct life cycle of luxury brands, with the revitalisation phase representing one of the primary challenges in the management of contemporary luxury brands that seek to stay relevant in the long run (Meffert/Lasslop, 2004, p. 937ff.).

Against this backdrop, it can be assumed that LBACs play a crucial role with respect to both the positioning and revitalisation of luxury brands. On the one hand, luxury brands further increase their distinctive distance (Kapferer, 2012, p. 66) towards competing (premium) brands and non-targeted consumers by capitalising on the strong social demarcation function of art (Bourdieu, 1979, p. 293ff.). The arts serve hence as an elitist multiplier (Meffert/Lasslop, 2004, p. 940) that re-emphasises the inaccessible territory of the luxury brand (Catry, 2003, p. 13) and stresses the latter's unique role as "a promoter of taste" (Kapferer/Bastien, 2012, p. 78). High-profile art collaborations accordingly allow luxury brands to stand out from an increasingly overcrowded market (Maxwell, 2011) and to gain valuable visibility by generating extensive media exposure (Chevalier/Mazzalovo, 2012, p. 211). The arts' ability to strengthen the luxury brand's exclusive positioning is even more important since the emergence of the luxury market through its successive democratisation and de facto dependence on the replicative rationale of industrial serial production requires the "upkeep of the myth" of artisanal production. By collaborating with the arts that embody the ideas of uniqueness and singularity, luxury brands build hence on most customers' belief that luxury goods would still be produced entirely in manual work and thereby effectively sustain their founding legend that is based on "the artisan (art-isan), the iconic figure in the imaginary of luxury manufacturing" (Kapferer/Bastien, 2012, p. 108). On the other hand, joining forces with the contemporary arts permits luxury brands to gain new relevance and remain consistent with their modern target clientele's requirements. Leveraging the arts' "ability to create newness" (Boche, 2010) thus prevents that luxury brands' traditional "quest for timelessness leads to creations so irrelevant to the present day as to be considered old-fashioned" (Kapferer/Bastien, 2012, p. 34).

Since the luxury brand represents one of the constituent parts of the concept of LBACs, it is accordingly assumed that the literature on luxury brand management can offer valuable reference points for the systematisation of LBACs.

2.1.2 Brand leveraging

Despite their relatively young tradition within the management practice of modern luxury brands (Michau, 2009), LBACs and their underlying rationale can be classified under more general principles of branding as they make use of strategies that are commonly known under the concepts of "brand leveraging" (Keller, 2003, p. 597) or "secondary brand associations" (Keller/Apéria/Georgson, 2012, p. 314). Both notions refer to the associative coupling of one's own brand with additional image objects "that have their own knowledge structures in the minds of consumers". The consumer may thus "infer that some of the associations or responses that characterize the other entities may also be true for the brand" (Keller/Apéria/Georgson, 2012, p. 314). Consequently, by linking one's own brand to other, potentially unrelated, but in any case extraordinarily strong symbols of communication, one aims at either further reinforcing salient brand features or lastingly compensating for deficient brand qualities (Baumgarth, 2008, p. 194; Berndt, 2005, p. 152ff.; Keller/Apéria/Georgson, 2012, p. 314). The scheme in figure 4 displays possible sources of secondary brand associations and highlights in colour where to locate LBACs.

Yet, while the associative link between brands and art/culture is usually translated into some kind of sponsorship relationship in the brand leveraging literature (e.g. Baumgarth, 2008, p. 205; Keller/Apéria/Georgson, 2012, p. 368), LBACs as provided in the above definition show more heterogeneous forms of appearance (Arts & Business, 2012, p. 5), ranging, amongst others, from product-oriented limited editions and capsule collections[27] over experimental video installations and artistic in-store performances to more conventional modes of collaboration such as cultural foundations, art museums and extensive patronage programs (Binlot, 2012; Chevalier/ Mazzalovo, 2012, p. 209ff.; Garratt, 2012; Kapferer/Bastien, 2012, p. 33ff.; Klanten/ Ehmann/Sinofzik, 2012, p. 8ff.; Kolesnikov-Jessop, 2010; Maxwell, 2011; Michau, 2011; Stelzner, 2012; Swengley, 2011; Tungate, 2009, p. 108ff.). In the context of this thesis, the concept of LBACs is therefore rather understood as a sort of co-branding between a luxury brand and an artwork or an art institution respectively as an endorsement of a luxury brand by an artist (Chevalier/Mazzalovo, 2012, p. 211; Foulkes, 2009). Especially the literature on co-brandings and testimonials is hence expected to prove fruitful for deriving significant attributes of LBACs.

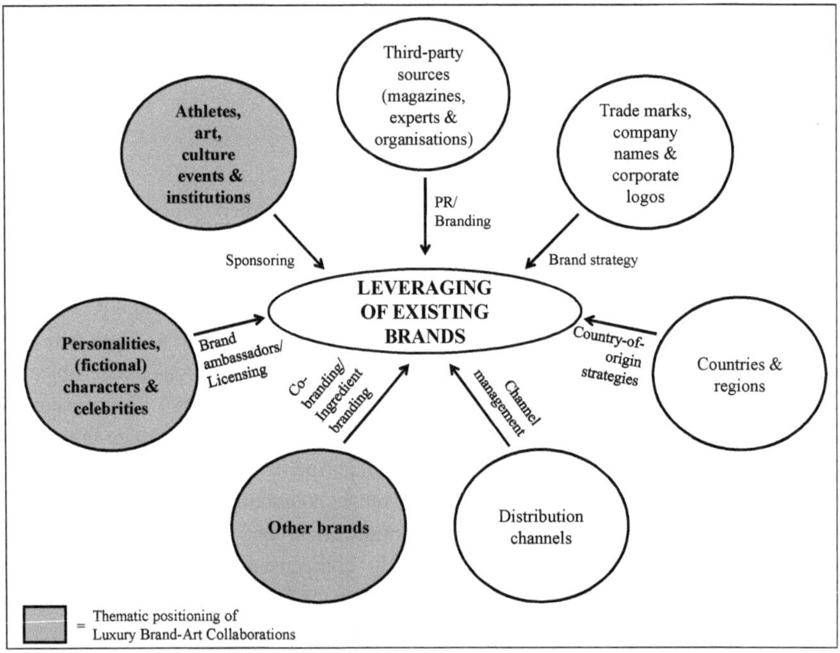

Figure 4: Sources of secondary brand associations
(Source: Own representation based on Baumgarth, 2008, p. 194).

27 Capsule collections are clothing lines made up of a few limited edition items that can be easily combined or interchanged. Nowadays, they are usually characterised by a co-branding between an haute couture designer and a cheap mass apparel brand, exclusively distributed in selected stores during a short time period and marketed outside both brands' regular clothing lines (Pennino, 2013).

In light of the above, it can be assumed that luxury brands seek proximity to the arts in order to draw on qualities, associations and consumer responses[28] that would otherwise be difficult to achieve through regular communication campaigns (Keller, 2003, p. 597):

(1) Creativity and aesthetics: Since the arts are commonly regarded as the epitome of unbounded creativity, luxury brands draw on their resourcefulness in order to entrench in the consumer's mind the perceptions of originality, ingenuity and inventiveness. The ultimate goal in this regard is to lastingly reinvigorate the luxury brand's innovative strength and capacity to inspire its target clientele's imagination by providing "proof of the brand's sensibility to aesthetics" and the latest debates on artistic issues (Chevalier/Mazzalovo, 2012, p. 211; similar: Boche, 2012; Kapferer/ Bastien, 2012, p. 34).

(2) Aspirational stories: By referring to the arts' creative universe, luxury brands can quite easily produce additional brand content[29] and further embed their narrative into an aspirational storytelling[30] (Boche, 2010; Kapferer/Bastien, 2012, p. 34). The role of brand content is even more important to the management of luxury brands since the latter are allegedly not concerned with the traditional rationale of positioning and its underlying comparative logic (Kapferer, 2012, p. 67). Rather, luxury brands need to offer an absolute universe that must continuously be refilled with authentic, somewhat secret and legendary tales (Kapferer/Bastien, 2012, p. 272ff.). By appropriating the artistic sphere, luxury brands succeed in charging their DNA with both new myth (Kapferer/Bastien, 2012, p. 37) and disruptive components that are the key to create and effectively sustain interest and curiosity among their target clientele (Fog/Budtz/ Yakaboylu, 2005, p. 81).

(3) Transcendence and social legitimisation: Through their linkage to the intangible arts, luxury brands eventually aim at being elevated towards values that transcend their purely commercial dimension (American Express, 2006, p. 9). By teaming up with the non-material arts, luxury brands accordingly signal their "capacity to cease thinking exclusively in terms of function or performance" and dissociate themselves from the

28 In this context, Braun (1997, p. 80) refers to "imagery-based attributes".

29 As opposed to the concept of branded content being defined as attaching one's name to content created by another party (e.g. by sponsoring an information or event produced by third parties), "brand content is designed and created by the brand itself" (Kapferer/Bastien, 2012, p. 269).

30 Storytelling as a marketing technique can be defined as the collectivity of rational, emotional, multisensual and narrative forms of addressing target groups (Dams/Dams, 2008, p. 30), and is meant to "endow any product of the brand with a good story to tell" (Kapferer/Bastien, 2012, p. 269).

material and profane character of luxury (Kapferer/Bastien, 2012, p. 37). LBACs are thus leveraged in order to "de-emphasize[...] the commercial nature of the luxury business" and to support "the idea that the function of luxury is the aestheticization of society" (Kapferer/Bastien, 2012, p. 108). The great attention that luxury brands pay to the arts today reflects in this regard their aspiration for social legitimisation through cultural commitment. The arts can therefore be qualified as the "social guarantor of luxury" (Kapferer/Bastien, 2012, p. 34).

2.1.3 Interfirm co-operation management

The recurrent use of LBACs in the luxury goods industry mirrors a more general trend towards collaborations at both the corporate and functional level; that is to say, over the last two decades, hardly any other management issue has caused such a great stir in both scientific research and business practice as the idea of interfirm co-operations (Schögel, 2006, p. 2; Sydow, 2010a, p. 1). The latter notion encompasses any kind of collaboration between two or more, usually both legally and economically independent companies that decide to join forces in some fashion with a view to gaining a shared competitive advantage (Sydow, 1992, p. 82). Interfirm co-operations owe their particular appeal to the (temporary) combination of the hierarchical characteristics of coordination with the flexible mechanisms of the liberal market (Sydow, 2010b, p. 375), thereby creating "the advantages of large organizations without creating the large organization itself" (Galbraith, 1998, p. 102). As such, the interfirm co-operation offers an alternative, if not the counter model to the vertically integrated and/or broadly diversified corporation: One refrains from having the managerial control over the entire value chain through the full integration of all economic activities (Sydow, 2010a, p. 1) in favour of gaining access to the strategic resources and capabilities of the partner company (Schögel, 2006, p. 3). Firms enter these co-operations for various reasons: They may intend to compensate for missing skills, expand their geographic reach, extend their product portfolio, build up or further enhance barriers to market entry, differentiate from competition or tap new customer segments (e.g. Bronder, 1993, p. 19ff.; Ernst/French, 1996, p. 166ff.)

LBACs show significant overlaps with interfirm co-operations in terms of their underlying composition, initial motivation, intended outcome, management challenge and diverse manifestations. First, both concepts exist since two (or more) largely independent entities have deliberately decided to team up in some way in order to achieve a joint goal. Second, irrespective of this particular goal, both concepts are generally about accessing skills and benefitting from advantages that would be difficult or even impossible to reach without collaborating. Third, in both cases, the common goal is often expressed in some kind of physically perceptible third element that has been either created from scratch by the collaborating parties, or newly composed based on existing brands, products and/or services that the partnering entities have brought with them into the collaboration. Fourth, both concepts entail the (temporary) merging of two different mindsets or (corporate) philosophies (Holzberg, 2009, p. 74ff.). Last, owing to the various opportunities for co-operation (Schögel, 2006, p. 3ff.), both concepts can take on extremely heterogeneous forms of appearance, thereby giving rise to the necessity to identify distinct types of collaboration that help to gain a better understanding of these crossover strategies (e.g. Schögel, 2006, p. 189ff.; Sydow, 2010b, p. 379ff.). It is thus assumed that the literature on interfirm co-operation management permits to derive meaningful attributes of LBACs.

2.1.4 Art-Business management

The current discussion on the stimulating relationship between the intangible arts and the rational principles of business management (e.g. Austin/Devin, 2003; Darso, 2004) has its roots in the idea of cultural management. The latter can be defined as the application and adaption of management[31] methods to the fields of art and culture (Bode, 2011, p. 161ff.) and covers all coordination and control tasks that enable and lastingly ensure the process of both providing cultural products and evaluating the performance of cultural institutions such as theatres, museums and art galleries (Hausmann, 2011, p. 32).

Yet, the question whether one might also reverse the direction of transfer and impact has, until lately, been largely neglected (Baumgarth/Lohrisch/Kaluza, 2012): By taking for granted that business-related principles necessarily serve as the ultimate benchmark for the management of cultural institutions, one has voluntarily refrained from examining the potentially positive influence that art may exert on the management of classic companies. More recent considerations on the relationship between the arts and the field of business administration thus try to explore to what extent art, culture and aesthetics can serve as a management tool, support employee development programs and provide a stimulus for internal structures and processes (Biehl-Missal, 2011). Company theatres, creative workshops as well as lyrical and musical interventions range in this regard among the most popular practices at the corporate level (e.g. Stollsteiner, 2008; Teichmann, 2000).

31 Pursuant to Drucker (1974, p. 17) "management has to give direction to the institution it manages. It has to think through the institution's mission, has to set its objectives, and has to organize resources for the results the institution has to contribute".

Pursuant to this new research perspective, recent studies in the areas of communication and marketing have adopted a more external view on the phenomenon of "art infusion" (Hagtvedt/Patrick, 2008) by investigating the impact of art on consumer perception, product evaluation, purchase intention, brand image and corporate reputation (e.g. Huettl/Gierl, 2012; Ringe, 2009; Schwaiger/Sarstedt/Taylor, 2010). Possible measures range here from corporate collections (Goodrow/Conzen/Salie, 2012) over cultural sponsoring (Bruhn, 2010, p. 193ff.; Emundts, 2003) and branding (Klanten/Ehmann/Sinofzik, 2012; Luna, 2009; Marquart/Esch, 2004) to art-inspired experience worlds, store constructions and events (Betz/Hitzler/Pfadenhauer, 2011; Herbrand, 2008; Nufer, 2007, p. 39).

The idea of LBACs thus takes its conceptual place alongside a range of existing research initiatives that explore the impact of art at both the corporate and functional level. The above research streams accordingly constitute the superordinate field of study, in which the concept of LBACs represents one particular research focus. Both the interdisciplinary character and diverse manifestations of the above interventions of art into practices of business, brand and marketing management are therefore deemed to provide helpful insights into the dominating collaborative patterns between luxury brands and the arts.

2.2 Deduced attributes of Luxury Brand-Art Collaborations

Reviewing the above theoretical points of reference has resulted in the identification of a preliminary number of 15 attributes that can, pursuant to their overarching thematic focus, be divided into four discrete sub-groups: 1. Attributes that characterise the luxury brand, 2. Attributes that describe the arts, 3. Attributes that address the relationship that both parties enter into in the context of LBACs and 4. Attributes that relate to the realisation of the concrete LBAC. In the following, the attributes will be both presented and described in their specific characteristic values.

2.2.1 Attributes of the luxury brand

Product category: Luxury brands can be distinguished according to the product category in which they primarily operate (Chevalier/Mazzalovo, 2012, p. 51ff.; McKinsey, 1990; The Economist, 1993, p. 91; similar: Schögel, 2006, p. 203; Sydow, 2010b, p. 380). For reasons of simplification, in this study, luxury brands can be alternatively assigned to three separate product categories. The category **fashion** refers to products that serve to adorn oneself outwardly and thus comprises apparel, shoes, lingerie, swim- and eyewear, jewellery, wristwatches, cosmetics, perfumes, leather goods and writing instruments. The category **catering** addresses both products and services that relate to one's physical welfare and aesthetic preferences and contains hence foods, spirituous beverages, furniture, home accessories, kitchen and bathroom equipment as well as hotels. The category **vehicles** applies to goods that facilitate mobility and consequently encompasses automobiles, motorcycles and yachts. This attribute is expected to show whether some product categories are more inclined to collaborate with the arts than others.

Affiliation: Luxury brands may also be organised into affiliated as against independent luxury brands depending on whether they belong to one of the "major operators" on the luxury goods market (Chevalier/Mazzalovo, 2012, p. 42ff.; similar: Kapferer/Bastien, 2012, p. 287). Whereas **affiliated luxury brands** are financially controlled by one of the three largest multinational luxury goods conglomerates (i.e. *Kering*[32], *LVMH* and *Richemont*)[33], **independent luxury brands** constitute single-brand companies and can thus be considered as "pure player"[s] in the luxury goods industry (Chevalier/Mazzalovo, 2012, p. 48). This attribute is supposed to indicate whether the practice of LBACs forms part of a higher-ranking, group-wide strategy or is rather directly linked to the particular universe and competitive positioning of an individual luxury brand.

Age: As a function of their founding year, luxury brands can be further grouped into old, middle-aged and young luxury brands. Based on preliminary random checks of the founding year of selected luxury brands (i.e. *Baccarat*, *Bulgari*, *Burberry*, *Cartier*, *Chanel*, *Hennessy*, *Louis Vuitton*, *MCM*, *Piaget* and *Prada*), for the purpose of this inquiry, it will be deemed that **old luxury brands** were founded before 1900, that **middle-aged luxury brands** were established between 1900 and 1950 and that **young luxury brands** came into being after 1950. Given the above reasoning in successive, time-related phases, the underlying rationale of this attribute alludes to the concept of the brand life cycle[34] (Braun, 1997, p. 55ff.) and the associated issue of a systematic life cycle management (Becker, 1996, p. 22). As aforementioned (cf. C.2.1.1), this

32 The French luxury goods conglomerate *Kering* was previously known as *Pinault-Printemps-Redoute* (until May 2005) respectively as *PPR* (until March 2013). The corporate rebranding followed a substantial change in strategy that had entailed the disposal of abdicable assets in order to primarily focus on both luxury and sports brands (Matlack, 2013).

33 *Kering*, *LVMH* and *Richemont* together hold a portfolio of approximately 1,000 brands, thereby accounting for roughly 10% of the total luxury goods market worldwide (Bruce/Kratz, 2007, p. 133).

34 Comparable to the concept of the product life cycle, "a brand's history [also] comprises phases of strong expansion alternating with phases of relative stagnation, and perhaps rapid decline" (Chevalier/Mazzalovo, 2012, p. 139). For a more detailed discussion on the concept of the brand life cycle see e.g. Bivainiene (2010).

reference appears to be especially important in the context of luxury brands since the latter are supposed to follow specific life cycle patterns[35] and thus require thoroughly adjusted marketing strategies at each stage[36] (Braun, 1997, p. 59ff.). Accordingly, this attribute is assumed to reveal which types of LBACs luxury brands enter in particular stages of their life cycle.

2.2.2 Attributes of the arts

Art form: Based on their particular physical manifestation, the arts are usually classified into the visual arts, the performing arts, music and literature (Baumgarth/ Lohrisch/Kaluza, 2013). Yet, since preliminary analyses of LBACs suggest that literature does not play a significant role within the context of luxury branding, in this study, especially the **visual arts**, the **performing arts**, **music** and **hybrid art forms** are considered. While the first three categories constitute established terms that refer to distinct and, hence, quite easily recognisable shapes of artistic expression, the comparatively young notion of the hybrid art forms represents an umbrella term for all kinds of artistic expression that entail the atypical blending of conventional artistic forms with the aid of new media technologies (cf. B.2.3 for more detailed explanations of the different art forms).

Role within the LBAC: Another way to organise the arts in the context of this study is to analyse the role that they play within the collaboration. As a function of the extent to which the arts are independent with respect to their creative expression, scope to experiment and freedom to take artistic risks, their role within the LBAC can be either creative-inspirational or functional (Baumgarth, 2003, p. 60). The arts' role within the collaboration can be described as **creative-inspirational** if the artistic contribution is not (or only very slightly) restricted by any commercial parameters stipulated by the luxury brand. This may be the case, for example, when a luxury brand asks an artist to freely design the architecture for its upcoming flagship store[37]. If, in turn, the arts must meticulously align themselves with product- and/or branding-related requirements, the

35 According to Braun (1997, p. 62ff.), the life cycle of a luxury brand consists of four distinct stages, namely the introduction, the elaboration, the fortification as well as the animation and control phase.

36 By building on Braun's (1997, p. 59) "normative life-cycle model for a luxury brand", Meffert/Lasslop (2004, p. 937ff.) detail both the phase-specific objectives and critical success factors of the management of luxury brands over time and put special emphasis on the challenges that brand managers face in the revitalisation phase of luxury brands (similar: Chevalier/Mazzalovo, 2012, p. 156ff.; Kapferer, 2001, p. 363ff.; Lasslop, 2005, p. 481ff.).

37 In 2000, the Italian luxury goods company *Prada* commissioned the Dutch architect Rem Koolhaas to create the brand's upcoming New York flagship store and let him have as much of a free hand in the latter's design as possible (OMA, 2013).

arts' role within the collaboration can be regarded as **functional**. An example for the latter case may be the capsule collections that *Louis Vuitton* regularly commissions from pop art artists: Even if these artists are requested to leave their unique artistic fingerprint on, and give a personal touch to these items, their artistic freedom is considerably limited by both technical and quality-related standards (Catry, 2003, p. 13; Radon, 2012, p. 108).

2.2.3 Attributes of the relationship between the luxury brand and the arts

Fit: The fit between the luxury brand and the arts describes the extent to which an affinity exists between both parties (Lasslop, 2003, p. 94). With reference to Nufer's (2012, p. 187) image transfer model, this fit is generally deemed to exist if there is a thematic coherence between the luxury brand and the arts. In this regard, Baumgarth (2003, p. 230ff.) distinguishes between three major levels of fit, namely the image fit, the product fit and the target group fit. In the scope of this study, the requirements for the existence of a fit shall be considered fulfilled if there is congruency between both parties on at least one of the above levels. As such, the fit can be either **existent** or **non-existent**. This attribute possibly reflects the extent to which a luxury brand, by joining forces with the arts, follows a "commonality" as against a "complementary" strategy (Keller/Apéria/Georgson, 2012, p. 317) or aims at an enhancement as against a modification of its current image (Klanten/Ehmann/Sinofzik, 2012, p. 8) (cf. "Image objective" in C.2.2.4).

Awareness level: The relationship between the awareness level of the luxury brand and that of the arts as perceived by the consumer can be either **similar** or **dissimilar** (Baumgarth, 2003, p. 59; similar: Maxwell, 2011). Yet, this attribute is problematic with regard to its operationalisation. While guidance on the measurement of the luxury brand's awareness level can be provided by the widely recognised indicators "brand awareness" and "brand knowledge" (Keller, 1993; Keller, 1998, p. 41ff.; Keller, 2001, p. 1059ff.), quantifying the awareness level of the arts appears all the more difficult in light of the latter's both highly abstract and divisive nature. Also, since it is impossible to determine these indicators for all LBACs being listed in the database within the time available, the final appraisal of both parties' awareness levels and the relationship between the latter will be made on a subjective basis, whereby a similar awareness level is also deemed to exist in case of minor subjective differences (Baumgarth, 2003, p. 59).

Direction of collaboration: According to the direction of collaboration[38] (Baumgarth, 2003, p. 58; Bronder, 1993, p. 66ff.; Nufer, 2007, p. 42; Schögel, 2006, p. 197ff.; Sydow, 2010b, p. 380) that both parties choose to give priority to, LBACs can be orientated towards either the luxury brand or the arts. LBACs are directed **towards the luxury brand** if the collaboration takes place within the luxury brand's proprietary universe. In this case, the luxury brand figuratively invites the arts to enter its commercial environment and to "do something inventive" with it (Maxwell, 2011). Limited editions, showcases or corporate architecture that have been designed by an artist serve here as illustrative examples. LBACs are oriented **towards the arts**, in turn, if the collaboration takes place within the arts' own ecosystem. Here, it is the luxury brand itself that explores new territory by entering the art world and providing the latter with different types of resources such as financial means, know-how in branding, public awareness or a valuable network. This support might take the form of cultural sponsorships, the awarding of art prizes or the foundation of art museums. Yet, the direction of collaboration does not refer to the direction of transfer of positive associations, qualities and consumer responses between both parties. The (mutually) beneficial exchange of secondary brand associations between the luxury brand and the arts is rather supposed to take place in both cases (cf. C.2.1.2).

Level of integration: The level of integration between both parties' contributions describes the extent to which it is possible to disaggregate the concrete outcome of the LBAC into the individual contributions that have been made by the luxury brand respectively the arts (Baumgarth, 2003, p. 61). LBACs show a **low level of integration** if these contributions are only loosely associated with one another in some fashion. That is to say, both parties' contributions are not intrinsically tied together, but are, despite their intentional link, still identifiable as discrete elements. This is, for example, the case when *Montblanc* sponsors a concert given by the Chinese pianist Lang Lang. Here, the individual performance delivered by Lang Lang can be clearly recognised as such whereas the luxury brand can boast at most the financial support that it accords to the pianist (Montblanc, 2013). LBACs show, in contrast, a **high level of integration** if the contribution made by one party becomes an essential component of the other party's contribution. The multimedia installation project that was curated

38 In both the brand leveraging and co-operation management literature, the direction or level of collaboration is commonly described as vertical, horizontal or lateral (Baumgarth, 2003, p. 58; Schögel, 2006, p. 197ff.; Sydow, 2010b, p. 380). Yet, these characteristic values do not prove useful for describing the direction of collaboration in the context of LBACs since the latter's interdisciplinary composition would eventually always boil down to a classification as lateral.

by the international video artist Leo Kuelbs for the champagne brand *Dom Pérignon* serves here as a case in point[39] (Stelzner, 2012).

2.2.4 Attributes of the realisation of the Luxury Brand-Art Collaboration

Time duration: Based on their time duration, LBACs can be either limited or unlimited in time (Baumgarth, 2003, p. 62; similar: Schögel, 2006, p. 195; Sydow, 2010b, p. 381). **Limited** LBACs take on the form of temporary projects, which are designed in a way that their termination is commonly foreseeable. Accordingly, they often materialise in the form of limited editions, capsule collections or seasonal store designs that have been conceived by an artist and are exclusively marketed respectively showcased by the luxury brand during a restricted period of time (Braun, 1997, p. 85; Catry, 2003, p. 13; Chevalier/Mazzalovo, 2012, p. 209ff.). **Unlimited** LBACs, in contrast, are organised in a way that their particular raison d'être does not imply their imminent end and may thus potentially be a sign for a long-term corporate policy that builds upon the arts as a constituent and identity-forming part (Baumgarth/ Lohrisch/Kaluza, 2013). Stationary art foundations, long-term cultural sponsorship programs or art prizes that are awarded by a luxury brand on a recurrent basis serve in this regard as illustrating examples (Chevalier/Mazzalovo, 2012, p. 211; Kapferer/ Bastien, 2012, p. 34; Tungate, 2009, p. 108ff.).

Number of parallel collaborations: LBACs can be further grouped into **single** as against **multiple** LBACs depending on the number of concurrent collaborations that a luxury brand enters into at a specific point in time (Schögel, 2006, p. 195ff.). This attribute does not only reflect the degree of exclusivity of the LBAC (Baumgarth, 2003, p. 62; similar: Schögel, 2006, p. 196ff.), but may also serve as an indicator for the level of commitment that the luxury brand shows in its cooperative behaviour towards the arts. Besides, luxury brands that succeed in simultaneously coordinating several LBACs have probably built up a considerable amount of know-how and expertise as regards both the organisational management and interpersonal handling of the artistic mindset[40] (Holzberg, 2009, p. 83).

---

39 In 2012, the New York-based curator Leo Kuelbs, the Hungarian video artist collective Glowing Bulbs, the German opera singer Nadja Michael and the French champagne house *Dom Pérignon* collaborated on a hybrid art project entitled "Divine Coalescence". In this context, a visit by the creative crew of the champagne's birthplace in Hautvillers followed by a private tasting with the creator of the *Dom Pérignon* vintages served as the initial inspiration for "Divine Coalescence". As a result, the brand's characteristic universe has formed an inseparable part of both the creative process and final artistic performance (Hugill, 2012).

40 This communicative expertise can be assigned to the concept of relational capabilities as part of the dynamic capabilities in strategic (co-operation) management (Lorenzoni/ Lipparini, 1999).

Intensity: Pursuant to the level of intensity with which a luxury brand links itself to the arts, LBACs can be categorised as either image- or identity-driven (Baumgarth/ Lohrisch/Kaluza, 2013; similar: Arts & Business, 2012, p. 5; Chevalier/Mazzalovo, 2012, p. 209; Schmidt, 2007, p. 35; Swengley, 2011). **Image-driven** LBACs primarily cater to the brand's external publics such as consumers, media, investors or competitors and can hence be qualified as relatively superficial and restricted in their relationship to the arts. **Identity-driven** LBACs, in contrast, are mainly geared towards the luxury brand respectively the internal processes within the luxury goods company itself and can thus be considered as both intensive and comprehensive in their commitment to the arts (Baumgarth/Lohrisch/Kaluza, 2013). This attribute accordingly reveals whether the luxury brand has truly assimilated art into its DNA or does only opportunistically seek proximity to the art world.

Image objective: According to the primary objective that a luxury brand intends to pursue by teaming up with the arts, LBACs can be divided into co-operations that aim at the further **enhancement** of the luxury brand's current image as against those co-operations that aim at the sustained **modification** of the luxury brand's present positioning (Keller/Apéria/Georgson, 2012, p. 314ff.; Klanten/Ehmann/Sinofzik, 2012, p. 8; Ringe, 2009, p. 26; similar: Esch, 2001, p. 245ff.). In order to reinforce its current image, a luxury brand may team up with an art form that shows, as regards its nature, role and/or origin, considerable overlaps with the brand's proprietary universe and exercises hence a both integrative and cumulative influence on the public perception of that luxury brand. In order to change its present positioning, in contrast, a luxury brand may join forces with an art form that substantially differs in its nature, role and/or origin from the brand's current image and has therefore a both disruptive and transformative impact on the public perception of that luxury brand (Kapferer/ Bastien, 2012, p. 274).

Brand visibility: This attribute refers to the extent to which the LBAC is visibly branded and can thus be clearly assigned by the consumer to a specific luxury brand. LBACs can feature an either low or high degree of external brand visibility (Schögel, 2006, p. 199ff.; similar: Kapferer/Bastien, 2012, p. 120ff.). If the luxury brand's proprietary logo cannot be recognised at first sight when looking at the concrete outcome of the LBAC, the latter shows a **low degree of external brand visibility**. If, in contrast, the luxury brand's logo is readily discernible at a glance, the LBAC shows a **high degree of external brand visibility**. This attribute potentially hints at the extent to which the luxury brand concedes to its artistic counterpart room for free creativity and has committed itself to the promotion of the independent artistic mindset.

Innovative level: The innovative level of the LBAC can be either low, medium or high and refers to the extent to which the actual outcome of that LBAC has been newly created by both parties (Baumgarth, 2003, p. 61; similar: Sydow, 2010b, p. 380). LBACs with a **low innovative level** are about co-operations where the latter's central object had already existed before both parties decided to team up. Here, the collaborative component solely consists of one party associating itself to a pre-existing entity that belongs to the other party and can be illustrated by the sponsoring of an art museum or a film festival by a luxury brand. In the case of LBACs with a **medium innovative level**, an existing entity is visibly modified by one or both parties and can be illustrated by the example of limited editions that usually comply with the constituent elements of a pre-existing product (e.g. brand name or logo), but visibly vary in terms of that product's more flexible elements (e.g. shape, colour, size or flavour) (Winter, 2009, p. 18). LBACs with a **high innovative level** refer to collaborations that entail the joint creation of a completely new entity and commonly combine characteristic aspects of both parties. In this regard, jointly created performances, artworks or fashion collections serve as a case in point.

3. Inductive attribute derivation

Prior to presenting the attributes that have been derived inductively, those case studies need to be discussed that have substantially contributed to identifying these attributes in the first place. Accordingly, selected real-life LBACs are subsequently briefly introduced before the derived attributes will be described in their specific characteristic values.

3.1 Case studies

In order to generate a wide and varied range of additional attributes of LBACs, the case studies must cover a broad spectrum of LBACs, with the latter being as heterogeneous as possible in terms of their strategic and operational orientation. The case studies were therefore selected based on the following criteria:

- **International representativeness**: Care was taken to avoid the selection of LBACs where the luxury brand always comes from the same country[41];
- **Structural balance**: Close attention was paid to the question of whether the involved luxury brands belong to one of the three luxury conglomerates. In

41 Yet, as most luxury brands are French (Interbrand, 2008b), a certain over-representation could not be entirely avoided in favour of the concurrent compliance with the remaining selection criteria.

order to mitigate potentially distortive effects, those LBACs were given priority where the luxury brands are either affiliated to different or no major luxury groups;

- **Coverage of several product categories**: Particular emphasis was laid on choosing LBACs that involve different product categories, thereby increasing the chances to obtain a diversified spectrum of collaborative patterns;
- **High degree of thematic variety**: In order to ensure the derivation of attributes that are particularly able to organise LBACs, those case studies were preferred that showed as different approaches to the integration of art as possible.

(1) *Chanel*'s Mobile Art Pavilion by Zaha Hadid: In 2008, the Iraqi-British architect Zaha Hadid has built a mobile art pavilion for the French fashion house *Chanel* that served simultaneously as a commercial store, venue for fashion shows and itinerant art museum, showcasing the avant-garde artworks of contemporary artists who had initially been inspired by *Chanel*'s legendary quilted handbags. Between April and November 2008, the pavilion had been travelling around the world's largest cities (e.g. Hong Kong, New York and Tokyo) before it was finally donated in 2011 to the Arab World Institute in Paris where it has found its permanent home in the unique architectural environment of this prestigious cultural institution. Since then, the latter uses the pavilion as a dedicated exhibition space in order to promote contemporary art from the Arab countries (Chanel Mobile Art Pavilion, 2013). The pictures in figure 5 show the mobile art pavilion at his current location next to the Arab World Institute by day and night.

(2) *Lacoste* x porcelain artist Li Xiaofeng: In order to foster closer ties with the Chinese consumer (Kolesnikov-Jessop, 2010), in 2010, the French apparel brand *Lacoste* commissioned the up-and-coming Chinese porcelain artist Li Xiaofeng to reinterpret its iconic polo shirt. As part of the brand's 2010 Holiday Collector's series, Xiaofeng's contribution comprised "one polo shirt made from 317 porcelain shards and one cotton polo shirt bearing a print of the artist's porcelain-shard digital collage". The well-crafted, one-of-a-kind porcelain shirt was – similar to an artwork in a museum – temporarily exhibited at the famed Parisian Hôtel Costes and exclusively presented to a selective circle of high-profile opinion leaders and upmarket clients. The cotton polo shirt, in turn, was conceived as a commercial limited edition of 20,000 exemplars and sold in selected stores of the brand (Zhao, 2010). The picture in figure 6 shows on the left the cotton polo shirt and on the right the porcelain polo shirt that Xiaofeng designed for *Lacoste*.

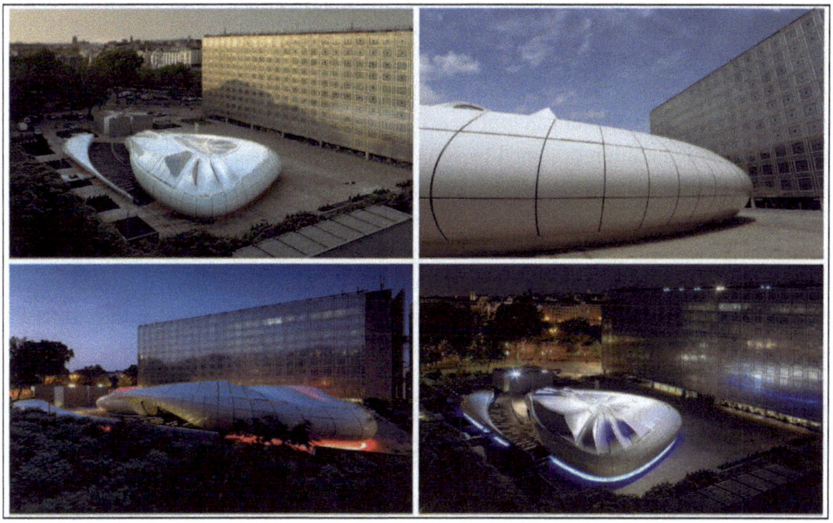

Figure 5: *Chanel* Mobile Art Pavilion by Zaha Hadid (Source: Designboom, 2011).

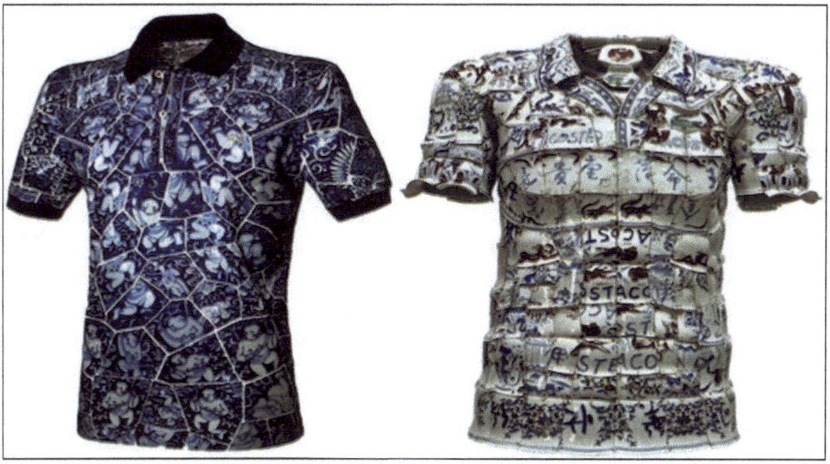

Figure 6: Polo shirts designed by Li Xiaofeng for *Lacoste* (Source: Lacoste, 2013).

(3) *Hennessy* x graffiti artist Futura: The French cognac brand *Hennessy*, which is a constituent part of the world's biggest luxury conglomerate *LVMH*[42], has traditionally been cultivating close ties with the contemporary art scene by regularly issuing special limited edition bottles designed by renowned street artists. After *Hennessy* had asked

42 The 'H' in *LVMH* stems from the initial of the cognac house *Hennessy* (LVMH Group, 2013).

the New York-based artist KAWS in 2011 to reinterpret the sleeve of its bottles (Chiu, 2011), in 2012, the brand's affinity to the arts reached another level of commitment with the 360° integrated communication campaign[43] "Wild Rabbit"[44] and the collaboration with the American graffiti artist Futura (Elliott, 2012).
While the limited edition designed by KAWS stood quite isolated outside the brand's regular communication platform, the association to Futura's artistic talent was fully incorporated into the overarching "Wild Rabbit" campaign. As a result, this comprehensive "multichannel collaboration" entailed not only the joint creation of a limited edition bottle, but also the production of two short films that were exclusively devoted to Futura and his creative universe, the launch of a dedicated microsite, an own tap on facebook, the inclusion of the artworks into the brand's then print ads as well as a costly launch event (Lamb, 2012; similar: Witt, 2012). The pictures in figure 7 show selected impressions of Futura's artistic contribution to the "Wild Rabbit" campaign, thereby illustrating the 360° integration of this particular LBAC.

(4) The Avant/Garde Diaries by *Mercedes Benz*: In 2011, the German automobile brand *Mercedes-Benz* launched the online interview magazine and global event series "The Avant/Garde Diaries" in an effort to both explore and promote the contemporary avant-garde. Accordingly, the declared goal of this initiative is to "disclose new ways of thinking and spread inspiration across all industries" (The Avant/Garde Diaries, 2013). The project consists of two essential parts that involve the merging of on- and offline elements: While the institutionalised digital interview magazine releases, on a weekly basis, inspirational short films in which artists from all over the world make statements on the status quo of the avant-garde, the long-term event concept features changing curators from creative metropolises such as Barcelona, Berlin, Copenhagen, Los Angeles or Rio de Janeiro that present their personal view on the avant-garde in different live event settings (K-MB New York, 2013). The picture in figure 8 shows the microsite of the project, which has been permanently integrated into *Mercedes-Benz'* corporate website.

---

43 In advertising jargon, the practice of conveying the same coherent brand message through all communication channels is commonly referred to as 360° communication (Horizont, 2011).

44 *Hennessy*'s current "Wild Rabbit" campaign, that was imagined by the New York-based agency Droga5 and launched in early 2012, intends a clear communicative demarcation from competitors' advertising by abstaining from showcasing the "trappings of success" in hedonistic settings that the cognac category is usually known for. Instead, the brand aims at connecting in a more emotional and authentic way with its consumers by celebrating with them aspiration and the pursuit of goals: "The campaign personifies the search for success as a 'wild rabbit', asking drinkers, 'What's your 'wild rabbit' before declaring: 'Never stop. Never settle.'" (Elliott, 2012).

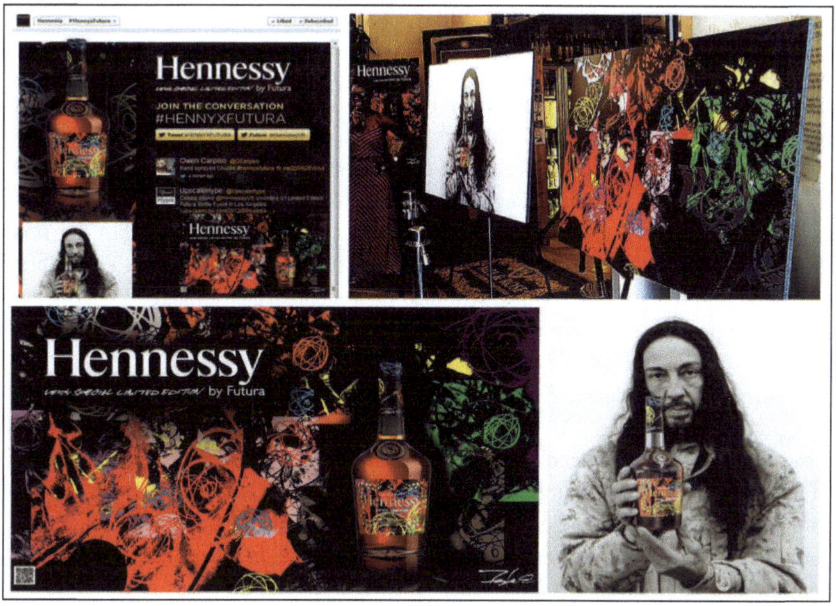

Figure 7: Futura's contribution to the "Wild Rabbit" campaign (Source: Hennessy, 2013).

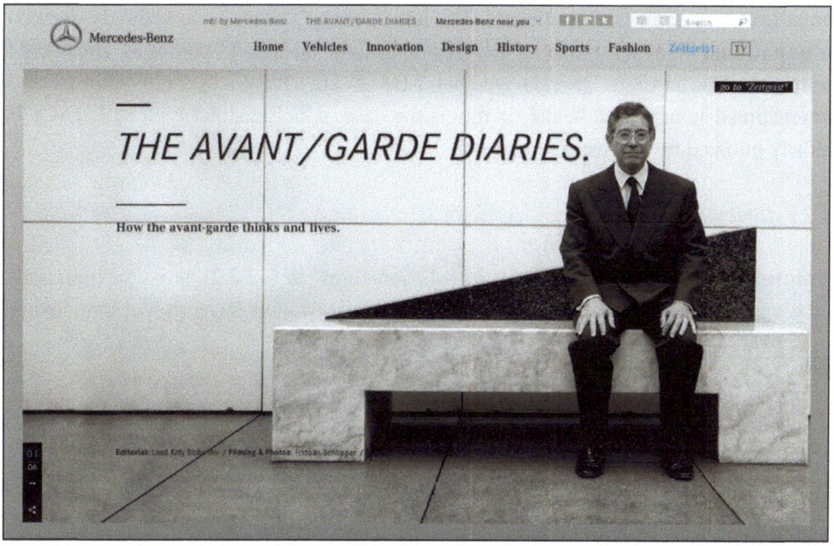

Figure 8: The Avant/Garde Diaries by *Mercedes-Benz* (Source: Mercedes-Benz, 2013).

3.2 Induced attributes of Luxury Brand-Art Collaborations

Analysing the above case studies has allowed for the extension of the interim list of 15 attributes by additional eight attributes. The latter will hereinafter be both presented and explained in their specific characteristic values. In order to better comprehend the inductive reasoning behind the derivation of these attributes, in the description of each attribute, it is stated within brackets which of the four case studies initially suggested the inclusion of the very attribute and its precise characteristic values into the final catalogue of attributes of LBACs. As was already the case for the deductive attribute derivation, the remaining attributes will also be systematically arranged by assigning them to the predefined thematic sub-groups or layers of attributes (cf. C.2.2).

3.2.1 Attributes of the luxury brand

Geographical reach: Depending on their geographical scope, luxury brands can have an either national or international presence[45]. In order to decide whether the reach of a particular luxury brand must be assigned to one or the other characteristic value, two, both easily manageable and verifiable criteria will be used. In order to be qualified as a luxury brand with an international reach, for the empirical purposes of this study, it will be deemed that the luxury brand's website must either offer more than two alternative languages[46] in the language selection menu or indicate major points of sale on at least two additional continents. The luxury brand's reach is accordingly deemed **international** if at least one of the above criteria is met. If not, it is considered **national**. This attribute reveals whether LBACs are entered by both national and international luxury brands and, if this is the case, which distinct type of LBACs is mostly initiated by the respective group.

3.2.2 Attributes of the arts

Nature: Within the different art forms (cf. "Art form" in C.2.2.2), artistic expressions may vary in their thematic nature. The above case studies have shown that luxury

45 Since all of the analysed case studies involve luxury brands with an international reach, it may be conversely assumed that also luxury brands of a more limited geographical scope enter into LBACs.

46 The website must hence be available in languages being different from both the language that represents the official language in the respective luxury brand's home country and English. Offering the latter is judged insufficient in order to be considered an international luxury brand in the context of this thesis since especially in former British colonies English still constitutes an official language. Although the website of the Hong Kong-based jeweller *Rich Jade* is thus naturally available in both Cantonese and English, the brand has not necessarily an international reach (Rich Jade, 2013).

brands seem to associate themselves with primarily three distinct qualities of artistic expression: Traditional, avant-garde and popular art styles[47]. Given that the decision on how to assign the different LBACs to these alternative characteristic values must follow pragmatic and readily comprehensible rules, it seems appropriate to describe **traditional** artistic styles as a set of creative expressions that are commonly recognised as culturally significant since they put particular emphasis on aesthetics, comply with high standards of artistic craftsmanship (*Lacoste*) and often deal with existential questions of life such as love and pain, peace and war or birth and death. **Avant-garde** artistic styles, in contrast, involve comparatively experimental, abstract and/or innovative creative expressions since they prioritise the free experimentation with modern materials, forms and themes over the strict adherence to aesthetic principles (*Chanel* and *Mercedes-Benz*). **Popular** artistic styles, in turn, relate to creative expressions that borrow their key themes from urban sub-cultures (Hill, 1976, p. 493) and thus mainly cover graffiti, pop and street art (*Hennessy*).

Country of origin: The arts can be further distinguished according to the geographical region that they originate from. Based on the insights generated from the analysis of the above case studies, the arts that luxury brands notably seek proximity to relate to either the **Western world** (*Hennessy* and *Mercedes-Benz)*, **Asia** (*Chanel* and *Lacoste*) or **Latin America** (*Mercedes-Benz*). This attribute may potentially indicate whether the strategy of teaming up with artists, artworks or art institutions coming from particular geographical regions is somehow connected with penetrating specific national markets or canvassing distinct consumer segments. To this effect, luxury brands may hope to gain a sustained competitive advantage in hard-fought markets by courting their most important customers and demonstrating a genuine interest in the latter's local culture and domestic art scene (Binlot, 2012; Kolesnikov-Jessop, 2010; Maxwell, 2011).

3.2.3 Attributes of the realisation of the Luxury Brand-Art Collaboration

Frequency: LBACs can be differentiated pursuant to their frequency or rate of recurrence into one-off, repeated and permanent LBACs. **One-off** LBACs (*Chanel* and *Lacoste*) constitute non-recurring co-operations between a luxury brand and the arts and thus occur only once in the luxury brand's history. The recurrent nature of

47 In this thesis, the idea of "style" does not relate to the strict definitions and conceptual boundaries that dominate in the area of the visual arts and intend to group artworks by the same artist or from the same period, location or school into distinct categories (Lindemann/ Boekhoff, 1970). The notion of style is here rather used in order to summarise similar artistic expressions or themes into superordinate groups for a better operationalisation in view of the typological study.

repeated LBACs (*Hennessy*) becomes manifest in co-operations that occur more than once in the luxury brand's history and may hence be indicative of an ongoing strategy in the scope of which LBACs are periodically reissued under the form of seasonal limited editions for instance. **Permanent** LBACs (*Mercedes-Benz*) apply to forms of co-operations where the luxury brand either maintains a constant relationship to the arts (e.g. art prizes, art foundations or art magazines) or enters collaborations with the arts that succeed seamlessly in time so that the luxury brand appears to be permanently involved with the arts in some way. This attribute is hence expected to show the extent to which LBACs are initiated randomly or, in contrast, represent a long-term strategy intentionally pursued by the luxury brand.

Form of appearance: LBACs can be further distinguished based on their particular form of appearance. Accordingly, LBACs that are, in the widest sense, product-related and thus involve the redesign of a product, brand logo, website, store and/or advertising campaign are grouped under the characteristic value **product** (*Hennessy* and *Lacoste*). LBACs that take on the form of artistic performances, sponsored concerts or any other kind of time-based art happening are summarised by the characteristic value **event** (*Chanel* and *Mercedes-Benz*). LBACs that succeed in becoming a renowned reference within the art world (Maxwell, 2011) and seem to be endlessly continued in time, thereby becoming a perpetuated or entrenched art-related practice, shall be assigned to the characteristic value **institution** (*Mercedes-Benz*). Annually awarded art prizes, periodic art magazines, stationary art foundations or art museums would consequently fall under the latter category.

Application: Depending on whether the tangible outcome of the LBAC is ultimately sold to the consumer, the application of LBACs can be either commercial or non-commercial. **Commercial** LBACs become manifest in for-profit forms such as limited editions, capsule collections or publicly accessible, but chargeable art museums that directly contribute to the luxury brand's monetary success (*Chanel*, *Hennessy* and *Lacoste*). **Non-commercial** LBACs, in contrast, materialise in cooperative forms that are not primarily profit-oriented (e.g. award ceremonies for extraordinary artistic achievements, corporate architecture that has been conceived by an artist or artistic in-store performances) and have, at least at first sight[48], no direct impact on the luxury brand's bottom line (*Mercedes-Benz*).

48 It is, however, conceivable that the presumably positive consumer responses provoked by the luxury brand's non-commercial association to the arts may eventually result in increases in sales.

Degree of 360° integration: According to the degree to which the LBAC is incorporated into a comprehensive 360° communication campaign, LBACs can be either detached from, or included into an overarching integrated marketing communication strategy[49]. Whereas **separated** LBACs are not featured in the luxury brand's usual communication activities and stand thus apart from the brand's regular dialogue with the consumer (*Chanel*, *Lacoste* and Mercedes-*Benz*), **integrated** LBACs are embedded into the luxury brand's overall communication platform and form hence an integral part of the brand's specific consumer approach (*Hennessy*). This attribute potentially reflects the extent to which the luxury brand believes in the arts' capacity to connect effectively with its target clientele and may thus be indicative of the degree of commitment and sincerity that the luxury brand shows in its relationship with the arts.

Consumer access: LBACs can finally be differentiated based on how the consumer can access and/or find out about the collaboration. LBACs that can only be accessed **via (corporate) communication** (*Mercedes-Benz*) commonly refer, at least from the consumer's perspective, to relatively intangible forms of co-operation such as patronage programs or the awarding of art prizes. LBACs that can be accessed **via the brand's regular store** network usually take place within the luxury brand's proprietary universe and may hence find expression in, amongst others, limited editions, capsule collections, artistic in-store performances or showcases that have been created by an artist (*Hennessy* and *Lacoste*). LBACs that can solely be accessed **via a dedicated structure** (e.g. art foundations or art magazines) are characterised by unique consumer touch points that stand outside the luxury brand's normal channels of communication and distribution (*Chanel* and *Mercedes-Benz*). The type of access consequently translates both the degree of proximity that the particular LBAC maintains to the luxury brand's typical target group and the consumer's ease of access to that LBAC.

4. Conceptual framework: Attributes of Luxury Brand-Art Collaborations

Following the quadripartite thematic organisation that was defined above, the structural attributes of LBACs, which were previously derived both deductively and inductively, are summarised in table 1. This exhaustive catalogue of attributes will

49 "Integrated marketing communication is a concept under which a company systematically coordinates its multiple messages and many communications channels and integrates them into a cohesive and a consistent marketing communications mix to send the target market a clear, consistent message and image about it and its offerings" (Lee/Park, 2007, p. 223).

hereinafter be referred to when describing the empirical cases of LBACs in the context of the typological study.

N°	Attribute	Characteristic values			
Attributes of the luxury brand					
1.	**Product category**	Fashion	Catering	Vehicles	
2.	**Affiliation**	Affiliated	Independent		
3.	**Age**	Old	Middle-aged	Young	
4.	**Geographical reach**	National	International		
Attributes of the arts					
5.	**Form**	Visual arts	Performing arts	Music	Hybrid forms
6.	**Nature**	Traditional	Avant-garde	Popular	
7.	**Role within the LBAC**	Creative-inspirational	Functional		
8.	**Geographical origin**	Western world	Asia	Latin America	
Attributes of the relationship between the luxury brand and the arts					
9.	**Fit**	Existent	Non-existent		
10.	**Awareness level**	Similar	Dissimilar		
11.	**Direction of collaboration**	Towards brand	Towards art		
12.	**Level of integration**	Low	High		
Attributes of the realisation of the Luxury Brand-Art Collaboration					
13.	**Duration**	Limited	Unlimited		
14.	**Frequency**	One-off	Repeated	Permanent	
15.	**Number of parallel LBACs**	Single	Multiple		
16.	**Intensity**	Image-driven	Identity-driven		
17.	**Form of appearance**	Product	Event	Institution	
18.	**Application**	Commercial	Non-commercial		
19.	**Image objective**	Enhancement	Modification		
20.	**Degree of 360° integration**	Separated	Integrated		
21.	**Customer access (via)**	Communication	Regular store	Dedicated structure	
22.	**External brand visibility**	Low	High		
23.	**Innovative level**	Low	Medium	High	

Table 1: Attributes of Luxury Brand-Art Collaborations.

D. Typology of Luxury Brand-Art Collaborations

1. Preliminary methodological remarks

The approach to the selection of attributes of LBACs has been discussed in chapter C.1. In the following, the precise methodology is explained by which these attributes will be empirically verified and different types of LBACs systematically derived.

1.1 Cluster analysis as part of the multivariate methods of data analysis

Since this thesis follows a typological approach that is both empirical and progressive and makes it thus necessary to identify meaningful combinations of attributes through the observation of real cases of LBACs, the performance of a **cluster analysis** is of the essence (Baumgarth, 2003, p. 49). Commonly referred to as **one of the explorative interdependence techniques**[50] (Baumgarth/Bernecker, 1999, p. 106) within the superordinate statistical family of the multivariate methods of data analysis[51], the purpose of the cluster analysis is to **systematise a number of objects**[52] (e.g. consumers, products or companies) by sorting them into groups that are as homogenous as possible with regard to their underlying attributes, and as heterogeneous as possible with regard to other groups (Kuß, 2012, p. 281). Market segmentation considerations **based on many different characteristics** (e.g. socio-economic, psychological or buyer behaviour variables) accordingly represent one typical field of application for cluster analyses in marketing (Iacobucci/Churchill, 2010, p. 506).

When performing a cluster analysis, several successive decisions need to be taken (Vogel, 1975, p. 46ff.; similar: Büschken/von Thaden, 2000, p. 344ff.):

1. Determination of a criterion that measures similarity within a group respectively dissimilarity between two groups;

---

50 In contrast to the dependence techniques within the multivariate methods of data analysis, the interdependence techniques do not distinguish between dependent and independent variables, but aim at detecting associations between variables and objects (Baumgarth/Bernecker, 1999, p. 106).

51 The underlying idea of the multivariate methods of data analysis refers to the simultaneous use of multiple variables on each object being studied (McDaniel/Gates, 2013, p. 542). For further explanations on the methods of the multivariate analyses see e.g. Kuß (2012, p. 235ff.).

52 Owing to its explorative nature, the cluster analysis belongs to the interdisciplinary field of data mining that aims at discovering generalisable patterns between a large number of empirical cases by processing complex data sets via computerised statistical routines (Kuß, 2012, p. 37).

2. Definition of a rule by which an object is assigned to a group;
3. Identification of the most advantageous number of distinct types;
4. Description of the derived types.

(1) Proximity measures: Proximity measures indicate the nearness (similarity measures) respectively distance (dissimilarity measures) between two objects (Backhaus et al., 2011, p. 399ff.). In this regard, two different levels of nearness respectively distance have to be considered. On the one hand, the similarity respectively dissimilarity between two objects with respect to one single attribute must be determined. This measure depends on the level of measurement that characterises the selected attributes[53]. Proximity measures are accordingly distinguished depending on whether they apply to metric variables (interval), binary variables (0/1-variable) or nominal variables (count data) (Backhaus et al., 2011, p. 400). Given that **only nominal attributes** are used in the scope of this study, two objects show either accordance (equivalence) or incongruity (non-equivalence) for one particular attribute. On the other hand, the different single proximities must be aggregated that two objects show for all considered attributes. This task seems problematic when the attributes feature divergent levels of measurement ("mixed-data-problem") (Opitz, 1980, p. 57ff.). Yet, as a result of a preliminary scale conversion, all attributes utilised by the present typological study show the same level of measurement. The following methodological comments are consequently limited to the alternative approaches to the aggregation of nominal attributes. The latter can be aggregated according to two different methods that depend on the number of characteristic values that these attributes possess. If all attributes have solely two characteristic values, the proximity measure for binary data must be referred to (Backhaus et al., 2011, p. 407). If, in contrast, some or all attributes consist of more than two characteristic values, **either the distance measure chi-square or phi-square** has to be applied (Backhaus et al., 2011, p. 409).

(2) Clustering methods: Clustering methods can generally be classified into either deterministic or probabilistic approaches (Bacher/Pöge/Wenzig, 2010, p. 19; Büschken/von Thaden, 2000, p. 341ff.). This study follows the **deterministic approach** according to which the assignment of an object to a cluster is definite and thus characterised by a probability that is either 0 or 1 (Baumgarth, 2003, p. 51). Within the deterministic approach, a distinction is made between partitioning and hierarchical clustering methods. Whereas one assumes a predefined optimal solution in the course of the partitioning procedure and tries to improve the initial solution

53 For further remarks on the different distance measures as a function of the respective level of measurement see e.g. Backhaus et al. (2011, p. 401ff.).

through systematic regroupings based on the different computing routines, there is no such best solution in the case of hierarchical clustering methods (Büschken/von Thaden, 2000, p. 351). Because of the progressive taxonomic approach applied by this study, a **hierarchical procedure** is hereinafter undertaken. As a function of the starting point of the hierarchical cluster analysis, a further distinction is made between agglomerative (each object constitutes its own cluster) and divisive (all objects constitute one single cluster) procedures (Backhaus et al., 2011, p. 418). Once again due to the progressive character of the chosen research design, one of the **agglomerative clustering methods** is adhered to in the following. In the course of hierarchical-agglomerative clustering procedures, the following sequenced stages must be processed (Backhaus et al., 2011, p. 420):

1. Starting the clustering process with the smallest possible grouping (i.e. each case forms a distinct cluster);
2. Calculating the paired proximities (i.e. similarities and dissimilarities) for all cases;
3. Identifying those cases that, based on their proximities, show the biggest similarity or, upon reversion, smallest dissimilarity;
4. Grouping those cases that are most similar respectively least dissimilar to one another. As a consequence, the total number of clusters is subsequently decreased by one and the paired proximities hence need to be recalculated;
5. Repeating iterations 2-4 until all cases are merged into one single cluster.

When calculating the new proximities in step 4, different procedures can be applied (Backhaus et al., 2011, p. 422ff.):

- Nearest- or furthest-neighbour (e.g. single-linkage or complete-linkage);
- Mean value models (e.g. average- or weighted-average-linkage);
- Cluster centres/objects of classification as representatives (e.g. Ward-, median- and centroid-based clustering methods).

The above procedures can generally be distinguished depending on whether they tend to merge the individual cases into separate roughly equal-sized groups (**contracting procedures**) or into few very large and many very small clusters (**dilating procedures**). Routines, in contrast, that possess any of these characteristics are referred to as **conservative procedures**. Furthermore, there are routines that tend to form chains ("chaining"-effect) and thus entail large clusters, which are only connected by very few cases (Steinhausen/Langer, 1977, p. 75ff.). Table 2 provides an overview of the most important clustering methods and their main characteristics.

There is **neither a distinct superiority** of one of the above approaches **nor a clear recommendation** for particular research situations. In light of the explorative character of the cluster analysis, it seems rather appropriate to apply different approaches within one and the same study design, to compare the results and to opt eventually for the most robust solution (Backhaus et al., 2011, p. 451ff.).

Approach	Characteristic	Proximity measure	Comments
Single-linkage	Contracting	All	Tends to form chains
Complete-linkage	Dilating	All	Tends to form small groups
Average-linkage	Conservative	All	-
Ward's	Conservative	Measures of distance	Forms equal-sized groups

Table 2: Comparison of the main agglomerative clustering methods
(Source: Own representation based on Backhaus et al., 2011, p. 431).

(3) Identification of the "optimal" number of clusters: As all agglomerative clustering methods start with the smallest possible partition under which each case forms its own cluster and end by uniting all cases into one single large cluster (Backhaus et al., 2011, p. 436), they do not produce one "best" solution (McDaniel/ Gates, 2013, p. 558). Rather, the individual researcher must decide which intermediate number of clusters can be supposed to represent the best possible solution in light of both the research question and design (Büschken/von Thaden, 2000, p. 362). This decision seems to be all the more complicated given the trade-off between the requirement for intra-cluster homogeneity and the manageability of the final cluster solution (Backhaus et al., 2011, p. 436).

Practical considerations, visual aids and statistical criteria may help to resolve this conflict (Backhaus et al., 2011, p. 436). Since the former are intrinsically tied to the interpretation of the specific outcome of one particular cluster analysis, only the two latter approaches can be discussed theoretically. Hence, when it comes to the decision at which level of aggregation the merging process should be halted, the **error sum of squares** (SSE), the elbow criterion and the so-called stopping rules are regularly used. The SSE measures the variation within a cluster and thus indicates at which stage of aggregation the level of intra-class heterogeneity of a cluster rises so abruptly that it appears appropriate to stop the merging process. If one plots the different SSEs against the corresponding number of clusters in a coordinate system ("scree-plot"), the visual identification of a flattening of the curve may serve as a further indication for the optimal number of clusters. The latter method is usually known as the **elbow criterion**[54] or "scree test" (Bacher, 1996, p. 247ff.). Eventually, statistical procedures, which are commonly referred to as stopping rules, may give additional hints as to the most advantageous cluster solution. The two **stopping rules** that are most often cited are the ones developed by Calinski/Harabasz (1974) and Mojena (1977). While the former compares intra-cluster similarity with inter-cluster dissimilarity and favours those solutions that show the lowest within-cluster variance and highest between-cluster variance, the latter assumes that the best possible number of clusters is reached when a predetermined value of the standardised fusion coefficient is exceeded for the very first time (Backhaus et al., 2011, p. 436ff.).

(4) Description of the identified types: The ultimate stage of interpretation involves the description of each cluster in its most frequent characteristic values and the assignment of a **meaningful name** that best summarises the distinctiveness of this particular cluster in comparison to the other clusters (Iacobucci/Churchill, 2010, p. 523) and may potentially serve as a tangible reference point for future research initiatives. Given that not all cases that are merged into a cluster show exactly the same characteristic values for all of the underlying attributes (cf. "fuzziness" of the typology in C.1.1), a **prototypical case** that best represents the structural characteristics of this specific cluster is usually selected and briefly outlined for illustrative purposes (Kelle/Kluge, 1999, p. 94).

1.2 Description of the research process

As aforesaid, the clustering of LBACs into distinct types is based on a hierarchical-agglomerative approach and will be performed with the aid of the software package for statistical analysis SPSS (version 21.0.0). In order to determine a viable cluster solution, the following successive stages must hereinafter be passed through:

1. **Collecting a substantial number of real cases of LBACs** and assigning them to the characteristic values of the 23 attributes that were derived in part C.;
2. **Describing the general sample demographics** in order to gain first insights into the potentially distinct profile of those luxury brands that are involved into LBACs;
3. **Reporting the frequency distribution of all 23 attributes** ("count data"): Attributes that are constant and thus non-varying because of missing or poorly assigned characteristic values are eliminated from the typological study given

54 For further remarks on the elbow criterion see e.g. Büschken/von Thaden (2000, p. 362ff.).

that they cannot significantly contribute to the process of clustering LBACs into discrete types (Baumgarth, 2003, p. 63);

4. **Deciding on a final set of attributes** that the cluster analysis can be based on and that must be reasonably composed according to the attributes' frequency distribution and belonging to one of the four superordinate thematic layers;
5. **Performing the cluster analysis**: In light of the overall positive characteristics of the average-linkage approach (Baumgarth, 2003, p. 53), the latter will be referred to as the main clustering method[55]. Because attributes are used in this study that show more than two characteristic values, the distance measure phi-square[56] (instead of the proximity measure for binary data) will be applied (Backhaus et al., 2011, p. 407ff.). In order to test the robustness of the generated cluster solution both the clustering method and distance measure will be provisionally varied for control purposes[57];
6. **Determining the optimal number of clusters** based on both practical considerations and the elbow criterion[58];
7. **Profiling and illustrating the identified clusters** for communication purposes.

2. Empirical selection and description of Luxury Brand-Art Collaborations

The following chapter describes first the method according to which the empirical cases of LBACs were initially identified. Secondly, some general remarks on LBACs are made based on the insights that have been generated from the assignment of the real cases of LBACs to the different characteristic values of the attributes that were derived in part C. This chapter thus lays the ground for the subsequent cluster analysis.

55 Even though both the average-linkage and Ward approach belong to the conservative clustering techniques, the former is referred to as the main clustering procedure since the latter usually proves most appropriate in case of metric levels of attribute measurement (Deimer, 1986, p. 76ff.).

56 The distance measure phi-square – as opposed to the alternative distance measure chi-square – is used given that it additionally standardises the data. Such a normalisation of the data is advisable if the frequencies are unequally distributed between the single pair-wise comparisons (Backhaus et al., 2011, p. 409), as is the case in this thesis (cf. appendix n°8).

57 This approach is consistent with the requirements stated by Backhaus et al. (2011, p. 451ff.) who demand that, when performing a cluster analysis, it is not only important to comply with the criterion of transparency by precisely explaining the choice for a particular clustering approach, but also to challenge the stability of the generated results by varying both the clustering method and proximity measure (similar: Iacobucci/Churchill, 2010, p. 522).

58 The statistical stopping rules will not be applied here since they prove most beneficial in case of metric levels of attribute measurement (Backhaus et al., 2011, p. 438) or under the usage of the Ward approach as the primary clustering method (Deimer, 1986, p. 81).

2.1 Used method of data collection

Since the setting up of a comprehensive worldwide database of luxury brands constituted the pre-condition for screening these luxury brands for potential collaborations with the arts, alternative approaches to the collection of luxury brands are subsequently discussed. The method that was finally chosen is thereafter described in greater detail before the procedure will be specified by which the real cases of LBACs were ultimately detected.

2.1.1 Alternative approaches to the collection of luxury brands

In order to compile a list that incorporates as many of the existing luxury brands as possible and thus caters best to the requirements of the quantitative study by increasing the chance of the final sample size of LBACs being as large as possible, three alternative approaches were available. The required data could have been gathered via information compiled by

1. **Luxury trade associations at country level**: The French Comité Colbert, the Italian Fondazione Altagamma, the British Walpole, the Spanish Círculo Fortuny and the German Meisterkreis provide the public with comprehensive registers of national luxury brands by means of their usually freely accessible lists of member brands (Kaiser, 2013);
2. **Brand consultancies and market research agencies**: Interbrand and Millward Brown regularly publish rankings and evaluations of the worldwide largest and most powerful luxury brands[59] (Interbrand, 2008a; Millward Brown, 2012);
3. **Independent researchers**: In 2011, the German marketing professor Klaus Heine built up the so-called 'World Luxury Brand Directory' that claims to be the first exhaustive database of luxury brands worldwide (World Luxury Brand Directory, 2013).

The latter choice was eventually opted for since the use of the first two indicated alternatives gives rise to several drawbacks:

(1) Lack of an explicit definition of the luxury brand: Except for Interbrand (2008a, p. 3) and both the German and Spanish luxury trade associations (Círculo Fortuny,

59 Many authors across the international luxury brand management literature accordingly refer to Interbrand or Millward Brown when it comes to collecting, ranking and/or evaluating luxury brands (e.g. Braun, 1997, p. 106; Chevalier/Mazzalovo, 2012, p. 92ff.; Kapferer/Bastien, 2012, p. 146).

2013; Meisterkreis, 2013) neither Millward Brown (2012) nor the remaining trade associations have drawn up an explicit preliminary definition of the notion of the luxury brand. Rather, they have merely established comparatively elusive criteria for being admitted into their exclusive registers[60], thereby impeding a clear and shared understanding of the used terminology. Accordingly, it cannot be verified whether their usage of the term of the luxury brand corresponds to the definition that is followed in this study.

(2) Intercategorical comparison with non-luxury brands: Probably as a result of the lack of an unambiguous terminology, the trade associations tend to intermix luxury brands with premium brands. To give but one example, the French Comité Colbert has recently accepted the German optics company *Leica* as one of its latest members, although the latter is commonly rather referred to as a premium than as a luxury brand (Presseportal, 2011). The exclusive reference to national registers thus bears the risk to indiscriminately mix up luxury and non-luxury brands, and to follow no longer the definition of the luxury brand that this thesis has initially adhered to. Interbrand (2012) and Millward Brown (2012), in turn, do not rate solely luxury brands, but rank brands across all categories based on their measurable brand value. As a result, only those luxury brands appear in these rankings that have the (financial) resources to compete on an equal footing with the largest multinational corporations. Smaller, especially family-owned luxury brands have therefore relatively poor prospects to be placed in the echelons of those rankings.

(3) Pursuit of divergent objectives: Neither the trade associations nor the brand consultancies have compiled their datasets for the sake of drawing up a comprehensive list of luxury brands, but rather in order to serve profit-oriented purposes: Both the representation and protection of their members' economic, financial and political interests for the former (Bruce/Kratz, 2007, p. 136; Comité Colbert, 2013; Meisterkreis, 2013), and the establishment of monetary rankings of the world's most valuable brands for the latter (Cooper, 2012, p. 2; Interbrand, 2012, p. 7). The principle of completeness, which is of an overriding importance to this study, is hence logically secondary to the above objectives.

(4) Promotion of national interests: Given that one of the declared aims of the trade associations at country level is the international promotion of their national cultural

60 While both the Fondazione Altagamma (2013) and Walpole (2013) cite highest standards in terms of quality, style, design, craftsmanship, creativity, service and innovation as requirements for receiving membership, the Comité Colbert (2013) mentions criteria such as international ambition, brand identity, creation, poetry and ethics, that can, at least partially, hardly be operationalised.

heritage (e.g. Círculo Fortuny, 2013; Fondazione Altagamma, 2013), most organisations grant membership not only to luxury brands, but also include theatres, museums and even landscapes into their member base (e.g. Comité Colbert, 2013; Walpole, 2013).

(5) Low level of representativity: Both the national registers and international rankings suffer from a distinct lack of representativity. While the trade associations at country level list almost exclusively national luxury brands[61], the rankings issued by the brand consultancies only account for the largest and financially most successful luxury brands. The popular recourse to such headings as "The leading luxury brands" (Interbrand, 2008a, p. 1), "Movers and shakers" (Millward Brown, 2012) or "World's most powerful luxury brands" (Sherman, 2008) reflects the orientation of these rankings towards a solely monetary valuation that is given priority over a representative, non-evaluative compilation of all existing luxury brands worldwide.

(6) Lack of comparability: The ultimate consequence of the above downsides boils down to a significant lack of comparable data. That is to say, if the first two alternatives had been selected as primary sources of information, it would have been necessary to combine different registers and rankings in order to offset the deficient representativity of the individual data sets. Yet, the latter are not directly comparable due to the divergent methods by which they were initially set up and the different underlying interpretations of the concept of the luxury brand.

2.1.2 Presentation of the 'World Luxury Brand Directory'

The 'World Luxury Brand Directory' (WLBD), which the German researcher Heine has initiated in 2011 in the context of his doctoral studies at the Technische Universität Berlin, constitutes a comprehensive database of luxury brands whose declared raison d'être is "to identify all luxury brands worldwide and to list them in this directory" (World Luxury Brand Directory, 2013). When this study was carried out, the database comprised 676 luxury brands[62] and offered registered users various filters in order to break down the total number of luxury brands into more refined classifications[63]. Within the WLBD, it can accordingly be distinguished between:

61 An exception to this is the French Comité Colbert that appointed in 2011 the German brands *Leica* and *Montblanc* as its sole foreign members (Presseportal, 2011).

62 Refer to appendix n°2 in order to consult the adapted list of 654 luxury brands that were screened for potential collaborations with the arts for the empirical purposes of this study.

63 Heine authorised the author of this thesis to access the restricted area of the WLBD and to use all available research functions within the database (cf. appendix n°1).

- **Different brand types**: Connoisseur brand, Little star, Big star and Star brand;
- **Different luxury levels**: Entry-level luxury brand, Medium-level luxury brand, Top-level luxury brand, Elite-level luxury brand and Ostentatious extreme luxury;
- **Different brand categories**: Luxury brand, Functional luxury brand, Discontinued luxury brand, Once-upon-a-time luxury brand, Blurry luxury brand, Luxury product brand and Wanna-be-luxury brand.

Compared to the shortcomings shown by the above registers and rankings, the WLBD produces clear benefits:

(1) Definitional consistency: Given that Heine's definition of the luxury brand, which was adhered to at the outset of this work (cf. B.1.2), has initially provided the theoretical foundation for setting up the WLBD, all brands itemised in the exported list necessarily meet the established definition[64] (World Luxury Brand Directory, 2013).^

(2) Consistent raison d'être: In contrast to the competing datasets, the WLBD does not pursue any third objective, but has been exclusively established for the sake of drawing up an exhaustive list of all existing luxury brands worldwide. Accordingly, both the nature and purpose of the directory perfectly match the requirements of this thesis.

(3) High level of representativeness: As against the alternative datasets, the WLBD is neither limited to any geographical zone nor based on restrictive brand equity-related considerations, but covers luxury brands on an international scale across all conceivable product categories and company sizes. The WLBD accordingly covers 100% of the luxury brands being listed within the rankings established by both Interbrand (2008a, p. 5) and Millward Brown (2012). As regards the national trade associations, the WLBD comprises 81% of the member brands registered by the French Comité Colbert (2013), 33% of the member brands registered by the Spanish Círculo Fortuny (2013), 65% of the member brands registered by the Italian Fondazione Altagamma (2013) and 41% of the member brands registered by the

64 The conceptual consistency between the theoretical definition on the one, and the functional database on the other hand is further enhanced by the underlying definitional logic. Pursuant to the difference between intensional and extensional definitions, the concept of the luxury brand can be subdivided into its intension (its intangible meaning or all criteria that decide about the affiliation of a brand to the term of the luxury brand) and its extension (its tangible constituent parts or a list citing all the brands that are covered by the term of the luxury brand) (Eckes, 1991, p. 21; Kromrey, 2009, p. 143). Accordingly, "the concept [of the luxury brand] determines the meaning of luxury brands (= intensional definition) and the directory lists the objects of this category (= extensional definition)" (World Luxury Brand Directory, 2013).

British Walpole (2013)[65]. At first sight, the partially low percentages appear to refute the supposed representativeness of the WLBD. Yet, in all cases, they can be ascribed to the fact that the luxury trade associations at country level do not exclusively grant membership to luxury brands, but also to cultural and political institutions, to nature reserves and landscapes as well as to publishing houses, business consultancies and law firms, which have nothing to do with the idea of the luxury brand as defined in the context of this thesis and are thus not relevant for the typological study. As a result, if solely the luxury brands within these registers are considered, their coverage by the WLBD accounts in all cases for nearly 100%.

2.1.3 Configuration and adaptation of the 'World Luxury Brand Directory'

As a prerequisite for the utilisation of the WLBD for the empirical selection of LBACs, one of the proposed filters must be selected. Also, the initial dataset must be adjusted to the requirements of the typological study. Both the configuration and adaption of the WLBD are hereinafter addressed in greater detail.

(1) Configuration: In view of the definition of the luxury brand that this thesis has initially adhered to and the purposes of the typological study, the basic register "luxury brand" within the filter "brand category" has been chosen. The latter was supposed to generate in all likelihood the broadest possible spectrum of luxury brands that might potentially collaborate with the arts and to increase hence the chances to bring about as many different forms of collaboration between luxury brands and the arts as possible.

(2) Adaptation: Initially, the WLBD solely contained the brand name and, in few cases, the product category, the country of origin as well as the city in which the luxury brand was headquartered when the WLBD was first set up. Also, the WLBD has not been extensively updated since its establishment in 2011. It was accordingly required to

- Check each brand name in order to ensure that the particular brand still exists;
- Delete those brand names that could not be identified on the Internet (e.g. *Euphoria*, *Bergers*, *Delta*, *Carnet* or *Vermont*), were discontinued since the database had been built up (e.g. *Sebring* or *Morgan*), were listed twice (e.g. *Christie's* or *Robert Clergerie*), rather constitute sub-contractors than brands (e.g. *Edgar Hamon*) or do not comply with Heine's (2011, p. 46) preliminary definition of the luxury brand (e.g. the manufacturer of safety footwear *Heckel*);

65 Since the German Meisterkreis (2013) does not publish a list of its member brands, the latter's coverage by the WLBD could not be calculated.

- Include brands that have, since 2011, been awarded the status of haute couture (e.g. *Alexis Mabille* and *Maison Martin Margiela*; Sowray, 2012), admitted to one of the national luxury trade associations (e.g. *Dr Irena Eris*; Comité Colbert, 2013) or acquired by one of the major luxury conglomerates (e.g. *Peter Millar* by Richemont; Mulier, 2012);
- Change the name of those luxury brands that underwent a renaming since 2011 (e.g. *Yves Saint Laurent* is now simply *Saint Laurent*; Cartner-Morley, 2012);
- Add the founding year, the product category as well as the country of origin for all luxury brands if they were initially missing;
- Verify whether the luxury brands belong to one of the major luxury conglomerates and insert an additional column for the name of the respective holdings.

2.1.4 Empirical selection of Luxury Brand-Art Collaborations

While the WLBD indicates the total number of luxury brands that need to be tested for potential collaborations with the arts, the precise approach to both the empirical screening and concrete identification of LBACs has not been specified yet. Since these issues are crucial to the required compliance with a **standardised method of data collection**, they are subsequently discussed more in detail.

(1) Approach to screening: Three alternative ways of screening the luxury brands that are registered by the WLBD were initially considered: The establishment of a direct contact to the listed luxury brands, the recourse to samples described in the academic literature or an Internet-based approach. Given the large number of luxury brands listed in the WLBD, it would have been inefficient to directly approach each luxury brand in order to verify whether this brand either currently is, or previously has been, somehow engaged with the arts. Even though the leveraging of literature examples seems more convenient (e.g. the sample compiled by Chevalier/Mazzalovo, 2012, p. 209ff.), it would not have been consistent with the requirements of the quantitative study. As already mentioned under B.3.1 and B.3.2, concepts existing in the academic literature usually focus on selected best practice examples (e.g. the artist collaborations by *Louis Vuitton* or *Cartier*'s art foundation) and/or limit their analysis to the emphasis of some individual forms of LBACs (e.g. limited editions designed by artists or art museums). Accordingly, it would appear that a comprehensive list of LBACs could not have been derived by that means. Because the Internet-based approach proved, in direct comparison, to be most efficient as regards the need for an extensive data volume, it has been chosen as the most appropriate approach to screening.

(2) Approach to identification: The second issue relates to the method by which LBACs should be detected in the course of the Internet search. Two alternative options were available: LBACs could have been identified as such based on either the luxury brands' own websites or the common web search engines. The choice was made in favour of the latter option for two main reasons. First, identifying LBACs via the individual websites of the luxury brands would have potentially required varying research efforts due to the different architectures of these websites. As a result, this method would not only have boiled down to an indirect appraisal of the communicative quality of these websites, but would also have entailed the risk of subjective bias by the researcher. Second, given that not all luxury brands prominently communicate their link to the arts on their websites, valuable empirical manifestations of LBACs would possibly have been missed. In order to standardise the identification of LBACs to the greatest possible extent, each brand name listed in the WLBD was thus searched for on the Internet in combination with two art-related terms: "Art collaboration" and "artist collaboration". Those luxury brands that generated a hit on the first page of the search engine were incorporated into the final sample of LBACs. The adequacy of this approach is even greater since the institutional definition of art assumes that an artefact (respectively a person or an institution) is considered an artwork (respectively an artist or an art institution) if it (respectively he/she) is referred to as such by an authorised body within the art world (cf. B.2.2). Transferred to the web-based identification of LBACs, an LBAC was accordingly detected each time that the collaborative behaviour shown by a luxury brand was referred to as "art collaboration" or "artist collaboration" by a credible source on the Internet.

2.2 General remarks on Luxury Brand-Art Collaborations

Before different types of LBACs will be derived, some general observations must be made regarding the demographics of the sample of LBACs and the frequency distribution of the characteristic values within the latter. Finally, those attributes will be selected that seem to be the most appropriate for performing the cluster analysis.

2.2.1 Sample demographics

The adapted database by Heine (2011) comprises 654 luxury brands in total. The standardised Internet search resulted in 106 luxury brands that are currently, or have previously been visibly collaborating with the arts (16,2%). For 23 out of these 106 luxury brands several collaborations with the arts were ascertained (21,7%) (cf. appendix n°2). The cluster analysis is accordingly not performed on the basis of the number of luxury brands that collaborate with the arts, but on the basis of the number of LBACs that were detected in the course of the Internet search. The final sample size accounts hence for 136 LBACs (cf. appendix n°3).

By means of a chi-square goodness-of-fit test[66], it is first examined whether the distribution of the characteristic values for the attributes that describe the luxury brand (i.e. age, affiliation, product category and geographical reach) differs if one compares the luxury brands that collaborate with the arts (luxury brands with art) with those that do not collaborate with the arts (luxury brands without art). Pursuant to the convention of defining the graduated level of significance as $\alpha = 0{,}05$ (significant), $\alpha = 0{,}01$ (very significant) and $\alpha = 0{,}001$ (highly significant) (Schlittgen, 1996, p. 311; similar: Hair et al., 2011, p. 368), the results of the chi-square test reveal that the observed distribution of the characteristic values for all four attributes within the sample of the luxury brands with art diverges at least very significantly from the distribution that would be expected given the frequency distribution of the characteristic values for these same attributes within the sample of the luxury brands without art. That is to say, in comparison to the luxury brands without art, more middle-aged and less young luxury brands do collaborate with the arts ($p = {,}010$). The divergent distribution of the attribute 'age' may provide first empirical evidence for the initial assumption that luxury brands enter into LBACs, amongst others, in order to rejuvenate and to reconnect with the zeitgeist (cf. A.1.; C.2.1.1; "Age" in C.2.2.1). It can be assumed that this motivation is potentially more pronounced for older than for younger luxury brands. As regards the attribute 'affiliation', relatively more affiliated luxury brands enter LBACs ($p = {,}000$). This finding possibly hints at the strong influence that the CEO of the respective luxury conglomerate exerts on the occurrence of LBACs (cf. E.1.). Also, since relatively more luxury brands from the fashion and comparatively less luxury brands from the catering sector join forces with the arts ($p = {,}001$), it becomes comprehensible why some authors restrict the scope of LBACs to the product

66 The chi-square goodness-of-fit test is commonly used to appraise how well a given statistical model reflects empirically observable data. The aim is thus to explore to which extent the observed patterns represent those that would have been expected under the respective model (Aaker et al., 2011, p. 415; Iacobucci/Churchill, 2010, p. 359ff.). Yet, as the frequency distribution of the attributes of the luxury brand has so far not been scientifically investigated, it appears problematic, in the context of this thesis, to refer to 'expected' as against 'observed' values in the proper meaning of these terms. However, given that the WLBD claims to be the world's most comprehensive database of luxury brands and that the sample size of the luxury brands without art (548 luxury brands) is comparatively larger than that of the luxury brands with art (106 luxury brands), the frequency distribution of the characteristic values within the former is provisionally referred to as expected data and that of the characteristic values within the latter as observed data. The goal in this regard is to generate first insights into the question of whether the profile of the luxury brands that join forces with the arts differs from that of the luxury brands that do not collaborate with the arts. Hence, applying the chi-square goodness-of-fit test serves here exploratory purposes.

category fashion (cf. B.3.2). Eventually, comparatively more luxury brands with an international reach opt for LBACs than could have been expected in light of the frequency distribution of the attribute 'geographical reach' among the luxury brands without art (p = ,000) (cf. appendix n°4).

The attribute 'country of origin' offers further clues to the geographical occurrence of LBACs. From the 106 luxury brands with art, 25% originate from Italy, 22% from France, 13% from the UK and 11% from Germany (cf. appendix n°5). The pie chart in figure 9 summarises the geographical distribution of the luxury brands with art.

In view of these figures, it may be assumed at first that the practice of LBACs constitutes a predominantly European phenomenon. When one compares, though, the geographical distribution of the luxury brands with art with that of the luxury brands without art by means of a chi-square goodness-of-fit test, it can be concluded that both samples do not differ significantly as regards the attribute 'country of origin' (p = ,117; cf. appendix n°6). The apparent monopolisation of LBACs by European luxury brands is in this regard rather ascribable to the general predominance of the European countries within the international luxury goods industry (Interbrand, 2008b). The practice of LBACs can accordingly be considered as an **international (instead of a regional) phenomenon**.

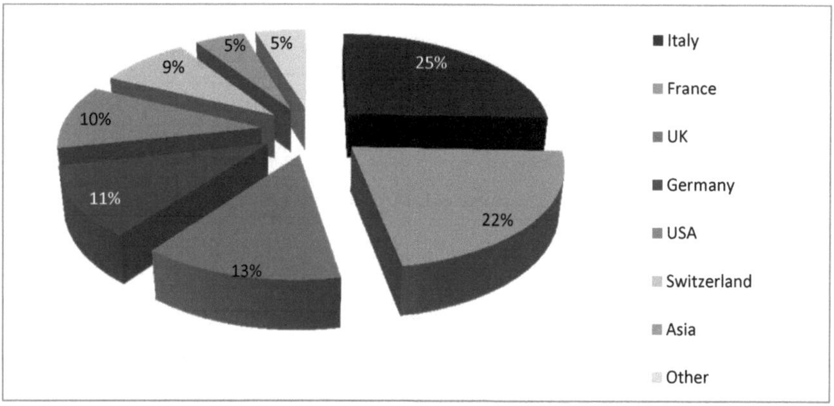

Figure 9: Country of origin of the luxury brands with art.

The analysis of the frequency distribution of LBACs over time eventually reveals that, even if the concept of LBACs does not represent a totally new phenomenon, the practice of LBACs has **notably grown in popularity after 2008**. Expressed in absolute figures and based on the respective launch date of the detected LBACs, the graph in figure 10 shows the evolution of the annual number of LBACs between 1984 when the first of all empirically identified LBACs was initiated and 2013 when this thesis was written[67] (cf. appendix n°7). Even though the Internet-based approach to selecting LBACs may have potentially distorted the frequency distribution in time of the occurrence of LBACs towards the more recent past, the overall trend depicted by the graph below generally supports the assumption of the "current art-luxe wave" (Maxwell, 2011) that was already referred to in section B.3.1, and further contributes to the relevance of this thesis' objective.

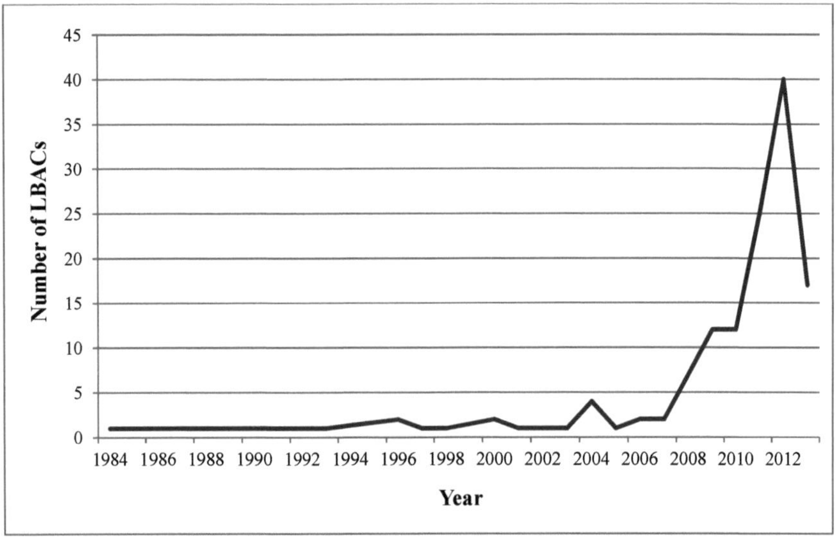

Figure 10: Annual number of LBACs between 1984 and 2013.

2.2.2 Frequency distribution

The assignment of the empirical cases of LBACs to the characteristic values of the 23 attributes resulted in a frequency distribution that is summarised in table 3 (cf. appendix n°8). At first glance, two occurrences appear to be particularly striking. First, the fact that the frequencies of the different characteristic values are fairly evenly distributed across the table supports the **high degree of heterogeneity of LBACs** that has already been assumed at the outset of, and gave the initial motivation for this

67 The sharp drop in the graph after the year 2012 is ascribable to the fact that the present study was conducted in April 2013. Accordingly, the annual number of LBACs for 2013 only accounts for the first semester of the calendar year 2013.

thesis. Second, the fact that the below table shows no missing values for any of the 136 LBACs underpins both the **overall pertinence of the attribute selection** and general ability of these attributes to describe LBACs in their essential traits. In the following, the frequency distribution will be shortly recapitulated, with the most important count data being highlighted.

(1) Luxury brand: While LBACs are mainly entered by luxury fashion brands (83%), they are initiated by both affiliated (33%) and independent (67%) luxury brands. Moreover, LBACs are equally implemented by old (32%), middle-aged (35%) and young (33%) luxury brands. Finally, nearly all luxury brands that are involved into LBACs have an international reach (90%), with merely a small minority being of national scope (10%).

(2) The arts: Even if luxury brands mostly collaborate with the visual arts (74%), they also appear to be interested in hybrid art forms (18%). Yet, both the performing arts (4%) and music (3%) are only poorly represented. LBACs integrate above all avant-garde (39%) and popular (39%), but also, albeit to a lesser extent, traditional artistic expressions (22%). Although more than half of all luxury brands assign to the arts a creative-inspirational role within the concrete LBAC (60%), in a significant number of cases, they express functional expectations towards their artistic counterpart (40%). Eventually, the arts that intervene into LBACs stem predominantly from the Western world (77%) and to a significantly lower extent from Asia (21%). Art that originates from Latin America, in contrast, is clearly underrepresented (3%).

(3) Relationship between the luxury brand and the arts: While two-thirds of all LBACs are characterised by a high fit between the luxury brand and the arts (66%), for about three quarters of all LBACs the rapport between the awareness level of the luxury brand and that of the arts is dissimilar (76%). Furthermore, whereas the direction of collaboration is in two-thirds of all cases oriented towards the luxury brand (65%), the level of integration of both parties' contributions is, in the majority of cases, high (88%).

(4) Realisation of the LBAC: The duration of the concrete LBAC is in most cases limited (80%). Moreover, while two-thirds of all LBACs constitute one-off projects (63%), one quarter of them are at least repeated once in the history of the respective luxury brand (25%). Only roughly one-tenth of all luxury brands are permanently involved with the arts (13%). About two-thirds of all LBACs constitute single and hence exclusive co-operations (68%).

N°	Attribute	Characteristic values			
	Attributes of the luxury brand				
1.	**Product category**	Fashion (83%)	Catering (11%)	Vehicles (6%)	
2.	**Affiliation**	Affiliated (33%)	Independent (67%)		
3.	**Age**	Old (32%)	Middle-aged (35%)	Young (33%)	
4.	**Geographical reach**	National (10%)	International (90%)		
	Attributes of the arts				
5.	**Form**	Visual arts (74%)	Performing arts (4%)	Music (3%)	Hybrid forms (18%)
6.	**Nature**	Traditional (22%)	Avant-garde (39%)	Popular (39%)	
7.	**Role within the LBAC**	Creative-inspirational (60%)	Functional (40%)		
8.	**Geographical origin**	Western world (77%)	Asia (21%)	Latin America (3%)	
	Attributes of the relationship between the luxury brand and the arts				
9.	**Fit**	Existent (66%)	Non-existent (34%)		
10.	**Awareness level**	Similar (24%)	Dissimilar (76%)		
11.	**Direction of collaboration**	Towards brand (65%)	Towards art (35%)		
12.	**Level of integration**	Low (12%)	High (88%)		
	Attributes of the realisation of the Luxury Brand-Art Collaboration				
13.	**Duration**	Limited (80%)	Unlimited (20%)		
14.	**Frequency**	One-off (63%)	Repeated (25%)	Permanent (13%)	
15.	**Number of parallel LBACs**	Single (68%)	Multiple (32%)		
16.	**Intensity**	Image-driven (84%)	Identity-driven (16%)		
17.	**Form of appearance**	Product (63%)	Event (20%)	Institution (18%)	
18.	**Application**	Commercial (52%)	Non-commercial (49%)		
19.	**Image objective**	Enhancement (68%)	Modification (32%)		
20.	**Degree of 360° integration**	Separated (75%)	Integrated (25%)		
21.	**Customer access (via)**	Communication (21%)	Regular store (59%)	Dedicated structure (21%)	
22.	**External brand visibility**	Low (20%)	High (80%)		
23.	**Innovative level**	Low (10%)	Medium (54%)	High (35%)	

Table 3: Frequency distribution of the attributes of LBACs.

The vast majority of all LBACs show furthermore an image-driven intensity in their commitment to the arts (84%). Whereas around two-thirds of all LBACs materialise in the form of products (63%), one-fifth take on the form of events (20%) and a similar share becomes manifest in the form of institutions (18%). Also, LBACs are in equal shares commercial (52%) respectively non-commercial (49%). In addition, two-thirds of all LBACs are meant to further enhance the luxury brand's current image (68%), while one-third of them aim at modifying the latter (32%). Three-fourth of all LBACs stand apart from the luxury brand's usual communication platform (75%), with only one-fourth being embedded into the latter (25%). The consumer accesses the tangible outcome of most LBACs via the luxury brand's regular store (59%), whereas he learns about one-fifth of the LBACs via (corporate) communication (21%) and can approach another one-fifth of them through dedicated structures (21%). Besides, most LBACs feature a high external brand visibility (80%). Eventually, around half of the LBACs are of a medium innovative level (54%), while one-third show a high (35%), and one-tenth a low innovative level (10%).

When analysing the real cases of LBACs and assigning them to the characteristic values of the 23 attributes, **two additional particularities** could be observed that are not directly reflected by the above frequencies. First, it is striking that the practice of LBACs occurs in quite restricted artistic circles as one comes across **time and again the same artists and art institutions** (cf. appendix n°9). To name but a few, conceptual artist Rolf Sachs, graffiti artist André Saraiva and visual artist Paul du Toit as well as the London White Chapel Gallery, the international art fair Art Basel/Miami and the New Yorker Guggenheim Museum have all already collaborated with at least two different luxury brands in the context of different art-related projects at different points in time.

Second, it is remarkable that some luxury brands have integrated the practice of LBACs into **comprehensive long-term marketing campaigns** (cf. appendix n°10). To name but three examples, the Italian fashion house *Bottega Veneta* initiated in 2003 the campaign "The Art of Collaboration" under which the brand invites season by season a different artist to shoot a creative commercial in order to sustain its avant-garde image and promote its bi-annual collection launch (Doc News, 2013). Likewise, the French champagne brand *Dom Pérignon* started in 2012 the series "The Power of Creation" that comprises two art-related initiatives. On the one hand, the brand regularly launches limited edition bottles designed by contemporary artists; on the other hand, *Dom Pérignon* organises, on a recurrent basis, events where artists from different artistic disciplines join forces in order to create unique time-based art experiences (Dom Pérignon, 2013). Similarly, the French manufacturer of luxury gloves *Causes Gantier* launched in 2010 the project "Causse Arty" that is about periodically issuing highly limited edition gloves in co-operation with graffiti artists, illustrators and performing artists (Causse Gantier, 2012).

2.2.3 Final selection of attributes

Since the total number of 23 attributes can be considered as being too large in order to perform an effective cluster analysis, it is necessary to choose those attributes from the initial attribute catalogue that best differentiate the various forms of LBACs. With the objective of assessing the different attributes as to their capacity to form distinct clusters, the selection of the final set of attributes will subsequently be approached from several angles, taking into account the correlation coefficient between paired attributes, the frequency distribution of these attributes as well as practical considerations.

(1) Correlation coefficient: In order to verify whether single attributes are significantly correlated and may thus potentially distort the outcome of the cluster analysis by jointly dominating the merging process, the correlation coefficient is calculated for all paired combinations of attributes (cf. appendix n°11). If two attributes turn out to be too strongly correlated ($\phi > 0{,}9$), it can be assumed that one attribute almost entirely represents the other. Since they would then be qualified as redundant, one of them must be eliminated in order to ensure an equal weighting of the attributes (Backhaus et al., 2011, p. 449ff.). Because all attributes show nominal levels of measurement, the distance measure phi-square is referred to when querying the proximity matrix in SPSS. Given that the value of the phi coefficient ranges for all 23 attributes between $\phi = 0{,}060$ and $\phi = 0{,}376$, it can be concluded that none of the attributes correlate so significantly that, for statistical reasons, it would appear appropriate to sort some of them out[68].

(2) Frequency distribution: Even though, at least from a statistical point of view, all 23 attributes seem to prove useful for performing the cluster analysis, the interpretation of the frequency distribution of these attributes allows for a more differentiated appraisal of whether all attributes are effectively equally suitable for the

68 Pursuant to the rule of thumb by Hair et al. (2011, p. 351), the strength of association between the attributes that are used in this study ranges between "slight, almost negligible" (for all coefficients between 0,00 and 0,20) and "small, but definite relationship" (for all coefficients between 0,21 and 0,40). Yet, the fact that the attributes do, albeit to a low extent, correlate must not surprise as the underlying rationale of cluster analyses precisely implies an association between the characteristic values of the chosen attributes. Otherwise, the formation of distinct clusters would not be possible.

purpose of forming distinct LBAC-types. More precisely, only those attributes should be retained that show enough variation on each characteristic value and can hence be supposed to contribute importantly to the formation of discrete clusters. Also, the selected attributes should be evenly divided between the four superordinate layers of attributes in order to avoid possibly distorting effects. That is to say, the more attributes are included into the cluster analysis that relate to a common theme (e.g. the realisation of the LBAC), the more the resulting cluster solution will be focused on that theme (McDaniel/Gates, 2013, p. 559ff.). The cluster analysis is accordingly based on the attributes 'affiliation' and 'age' from the layer that caters to the luxury brand, the attributes 'form'[69] and 'role within the LBAC' from the layer that addresses the arts and the attributes 'fit' and 'direction of collaboration' from the lawyer that refers to the relationship between both parties.

(3) Practical considerations: Given the comparatively larger number of attributes within the layer that describes the realisation of the concrete LBAC, the mere reference to the frequencies does not prove sufficient in order to decide on the final selection of attributes from that layer. In this regard, rather practical considerations may help to decide on which attributes are the most meaningful for the purposes of the cluster analysis (Backhaus et al., 2011, p. 449). First, the number of attributes from this last layer must not substantially exceed the number of attributes that were retained from the first three layers. Otherwise, the group of attributes from the fourth layer would dominate the merging process and, as a result, the composition of the final cluster solution (McDaniel/Gates, 2013, p. 559ff.). Accordingly, at most three out of the 11 attributes from the layer that relates to the LBAC should be selected. Second, in light of the reduced number of attributes that the cluster analysis is ideally based on, it is all the more vital that these attributes are best able to structurally describe the concrete realisation of LBACs. That is to say, even if all attributes were initially selected due to their overall ability to specify the concept of LBACs, it can be assumed that some attributes are more fundamental than others. This qualitative selection criterion is even more important since there does not exist any prior empirical research on LBACs. Consequently, instead of selecting attributes that refer to the detailed

69 Although the frequencies of the attribute 'nature' are more evenly distributed than those of the attribute 'form', the latter will be included into the cluster analysis owing to its better ability to form equally sized clusters. That is to say, after having merged the characteristic values 'performing arts', 'music' and 'hybrid forms' into the new characteristic value 'non-visual arts', some preliminary cluster analyses were performed for testing purposes. With all other selected attributes being hold constant except for the attributes 'nature' and 'form', both test runs suggested a 3-cluster solution. Yet, while the test run that included the attribute 'nature' resulted into two extremely large clusters and one comparatively smaller cluster, the test run that integrated instead the attribute 'form' brought about three rather equally sized clusters (cf. appendix n°12).

design of the LBAC ('form of appearance', 'image objective', 'degree of 360° integration', 'customer access', 'external brand visibility' and 'innovative level') or the collaborative behaviour of the luxury brand ('frequency' and 'number of parallel LBACs'), those attributes should rather be retained that address the most basic traits of LBACs while concurrently describing the latter in as much detail as possible. As this is especially the case for the attributes 'duration', 'intensity' and 'application', these three attributes from the fourth layer are used when subsequently performing the cluster analysis.

3. Determination of different types of Luxury Brand-Art Collaborations

Based on the preceding selection of the final set of attributes, in the following, the goal will be to identify distinct types of LBACs, to describe the latter in their most frequent characteristic values and to outline prototypical cases for each LBAC-type.

3.1 Empirical identification

Since the data set of LBACs does not contain any missing values (cf. appendix n°13), all 136 empirical cases of LBACs can be used for the purposes of the cluster analysis. As already mentioned above (cf. D.1.2), both the elbow criterion (contingent on the error sum of squares, which is provided in the column labelled "Coefficients" within the agglomeration schedule in SPSS; cf. appendix n°14) and practical considerations are referred to in order to determine the optimal number of clusters. Accordingly, the graph in figure 11 illustrates the relationship between the number of clusters and the respective level of dissimilarity (cf. appendix n°15). The curve shows a sharp bend at the transition from four to three clusters (increase: 0,015 units) as well as at the transition from two to one cluster (increase: 0,02 units). Due to practical considerations (merging the 136 empirical cases of LBACs into three clusters instead of into one single cluster appears more appropriate in light of the above-stated heterogeneity of the concept of LBACs) and the fact that, at the last stage of aggregation, the measure of heterogeneity generally substantially increases (since all different manifestations of LBACs are now merged into one large cluster), the **3-cluster solution** is tentatively retained.

In order to test the robustness of the 3-cluster solution (cf. appendix n°14), the cluster analysis is thereafter rerun several times, in each case with slightly modified settings. Based on the Ward clustering approach[70], the first trial run confirms the outcome of

70 In order to test the results of the initial cluster analysis, only the Ward approach is used since it constitutes the only alternative clustering method that is based on the same (i.e. conservative)

the first cluster analysis given that it suggests a 3-cluster solution as well, results in almost similarly sized clusters (cluster 1 = 56; cluster 2 = 47; cluster 3 = 33) and generally assigns the 136 empirical cases of LBACs to the same clusters as did the cluster analysis under the average-linkage approach (solely nine cases are assigned to different clusters, which corresponds to a rate of congruency of 93,4%) (cf. appendix n 16).

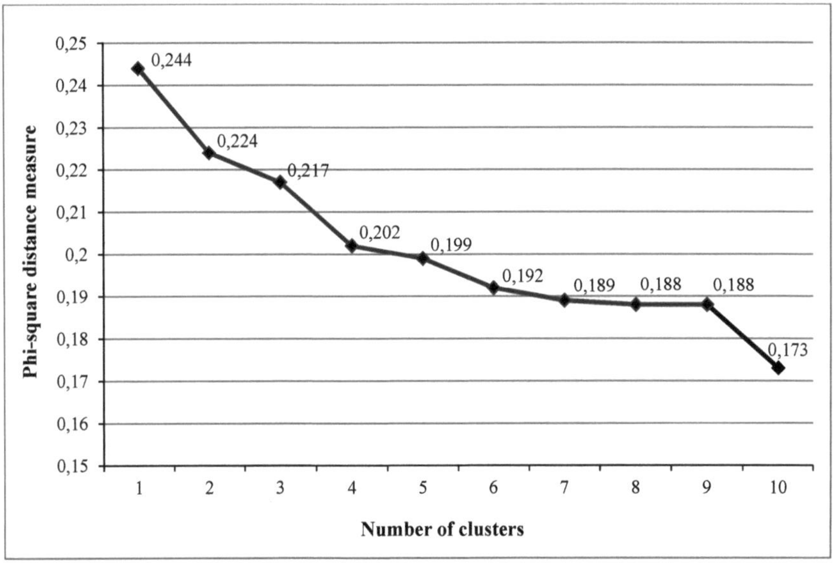

Figure 11: Link between the heterogeneity measure and the number of clusters (Scree plot).

The initial cluster solution is additionally challenged by temporarily changing the distance measure. Based on the alternative distance measure chi-square, the second trial run equally confirms the outcome of the first cluster analysis since it indicates not only a 3-cluster solution with similarly sized clusters (cluster 1 = 63; cluster 2 = 49; cluster 3 = 24), but also assigns the 136 empirical cases of LBACs to the same clusters as did the cluster analysis based on the distance measure phi-square (only seven cases are assigned to different clusters, which equates to a rate of congruency of 94,9%) (cf. appendix n 17). The validity of the 3-cluster solution is ultimately questioned by successively replacing single attributes for each of the four layers. In this regard, the preliminary 3-cluster solution proves robust for four randomly selected, isolated

aggregative logic as the average-linkage clustering approach and accordingly produces results that are best comparable with those generated by the average-linkage clustering approach. Also, the Ward technique is commonly recognised for its ability to identify reasonable partitions and to signal the appropriate number of clusters (Bergs, 1981, p. 97).

replacement routines[71] (cf. appendix n 18). In light of the sound results of the above robustness checks, the initial 3-cluster solution can be deemed to be sufficiently viable in order to be kept as final typology of LBACs.

In order to specify more clearly the chosen 3-cluster solution, a descriptive analysis is subsequently carried out using cross tabulations[72] (cf. appendix n 19). The characteristic values for which the respective cluster shows the highest frequency are kept as typical features of this cluster. If two characteristic values show similarly high frequencies for one and the same attribute, both of them are retained as distinctive for this particular cluster. By means of a chi-square test, it is furthermore assessed to which extent the selected attributes can be considered as being effective in distinguishing the determined LBAC-types (the number of * indicates the level of significance of the chi-square test) (cf. appendix 19). Moreover, by interpreting its most pronounced characteristic values, each cluster is given a both plausible and visual name. Finally, the precise size of each cluster is calculated (cf. appendix n 14). Table 4 summarises the outcome of these analyses.

3.2 Conceptual description

In order to lay the ground for a potential future conceptualisation of LBACs, the above-identified types of collaboration between luxury brands and the arts are hereinafter further elucidated, with their constituent characteristic values being especially emphasised and logically linked to one another.

(1) Arty Limited Edition: As its name suggests, the type 'Arty Limited Edition' is restricted in time and supply, takes place within the luxury brand's proprietary universe since being directed towards the luxury brand and is characterised by an image-driven commitment to the arts. Because it serves essentially commercial and hence profit-making purposes, the 'Arty Limited Edition' is, on a regular basis, available for purchase by the consumer. The arts accordingly assume a functional role within this LBAC-type and take typically the form of visual creative expressions that are somehow merged with a pre-existing product. The fit between the luxury brand and the arts is either existent or non-existent. Representing the biggest and thus most

71 The fact that the 3-cluster solution does not prove robust for all attribute replacements can be ascribed to the underlying ambiguous rationale of the explorative approaches within the multivariate methods of data analysis. Accordingly, there is no one single correct solution, but rather several possible solutions whose appraisal is subject to practical considerations as to the given object of investigation, the chosen study design and the individual researcher's interpretation (Backhaus et al., 2011, p. 452).

72 For further remarks on the concept of cross tabulation (that is sometimes also referred to as contingency table analysis) see e.g. Backhaus et al. (2011, p. 303ff.).

widespread of the three clusters, the 'Arty Limited Edition' is principally launched by independent and old luxury brands.

	Cluster 1	Cluster 2	Cluster 3
Name	**Arty Limited Edition**	**Philanthropic LBAC**	**Experimental LBAC**
Affiliation	Independent (71%)	Affiliated (43%)/ Independent (57%)	Independent (76%)
Age***	Old (43%)	Middle-aged (43%)	Young (76%)
Form**	Visual arts (88%)	Visual arts (67%)/ Non-visual arts (33%)	Visual arts (62%)/ Non-visual arts (38%)
Role within the LBAC***	Functional (93%)	Creative-inspirational (98%)	Creative-inspirational (93%)
Fit***	Existent (48%)/ Non-existent (52%)	Existent (84%)	Existent (69%)
Direction of collaboration***	Towards brand (100%)	Towards art (90%)	Towards brand (93%)
Duration***	Limited (100%)	Limited (47%)/ Unlimited (53%)	Limited (100%)
Intensity***	Image-driven (100%)	Image-driven (75%)	Image-driven (69%)/ Identity-driven (31%)
Application***	Commercial (98%)	Non-commercial (88%)	Commercial (31%)/ Non-commercial (69%)
Size	**56**	**51**	**29**

Table 4: LBAC-types (3-cluster solution).

(2) Philanthropic LBAC: The type 'Philanthropic LBAC' usually involves some kind of voluntary cultural commitment by the luxury brand, occurs within the art world since being primarily directed towards the arts and is normally not subject to any commercial or profit-making purposes. The arts are therefore given the freedom to materialise in creative-inspirational expressions that can be of either visual or non-visual nature. While the 'Philanthropic LBAC' shows a predominantly image-driven intensity in its relationship to the arts, it can be either limited or unlimited in time.

There is furthermore commonly a fit between the luxury brand and the arts. Constituting the second biggest LBAC-type, the 'Philanthropic LBAC' is initiated by both affiliated and independent luxury brands and is particularly entered by middle-aged luxury brands.

(3) Experimental LBAC: The type 'Experimental LBAC' characteristically features a large room for manoeuvre that the luxury brand and the arts agree on in order to come up with unparalleled creative cross-over ventures. Being notably entered by independent and young luxury brands together with a fitting artistic counterpart, this LBAC-type is generally limited in time, but can have an either image- or identity-driven commitment to the arts. While the 'Experimental LBAC' is regularly oriented towards the luxury brand, it can serve both commercial and non-commercial purposes. Yet, as the label of this collaborative type implies, the arts are accorded the necessary freedom to experiment, thus play in any case a creative-inspirational role within the LBAC and are consequently not confined to any specific art form. The 'Experimental LBAC' represents the smallest of the three clusters.

3.3 Prototypical cases

In order to illustrate the tripartite typology of LBACs, prototypical cases for each cluster are subsequently briefly outlined. Since for each cluster an empirical case was selected that concurs with all of the characteristic values for which this cluster shows the highest frequency, the below examples are assumed to best represent the typology of LBACs.

(1) *Hermès* "Graff" collection by Kongo: In 2011, the French luxury brand *Hermès* commissioned the French-Vietnamese graffiti artist Cyril Phan, who is internationally better known by his artistic pseudonym Kongo, to reinterpret its signature scarves. Labelled "*Hermès* Graff by Kongo" and restricted in time to the Fall/Winter collection 2011-2012, the joint project gave birth to a highly publicised limited edition collection. The latter comprised six different silk scarves that were embellished by the artist with colourful tag-style prints and featured the brand's name in lively bubble letters (Maeland, 2011). Yet, although the artist was asked to leave his unique artistic fingerprint on, and add a personal touch to the product, he had to comply with product-related requirements such as the use of the characteristic silk material and the observance of the proprietary form of the scarves. The pictures in figure 12 show one of the scarves designed by Kongo as well as the artist himself standing in front of the *Hermès* flagship store in Barcelona and creating a giant piece of graffiti on one of the brand's hoardings at the latest *Hermès* store opening in Singapore (De Villiers, 2011).

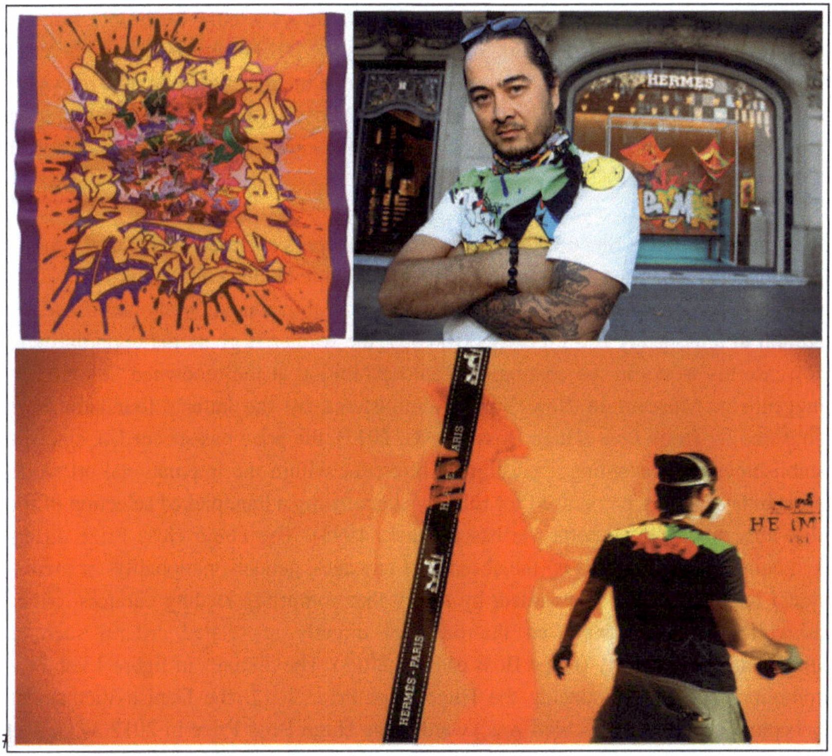

Figure 12: Impressions of the Arty Limited Edition by Kongo for *Hermès* (Source: Kent, 2012; Pak, 2011).

The scarf collection was exclusively sold in selected stores during a short period of time and artistically staged in dedicated showcases designed by the artist. *Hermès* donated a portion of the proceeds of the sales to Kongo's non-profit collective Kosmopolis, which is dedicated to supporting young up-and-coming street artists (Maeland, 2011).

Established in 1837 as an independent family business and constituting, ever since, one of the oldest luxury brands from France (La Tribune, 2013), *Hermès* can be supposed to have deliberately opted for a young, urban and rebellious street artist who is not in line with the brand's traditional image, but rather provides the brand with a more contemporary and progressive appeal (Maeland, 2011). Since street art represents the epitome of the anti-establishment revolt and thereby the contrary of the label's otherwise carefully monitored reputation (Elite Choice, 2011; Hamza, 2012;

similar: Klanten/Ehmann/Sinofzik, 2012, p. 27), *Hermès*, by temporarily integrating a representative of the "outsider art" scene (Bezuglov, 2013) into its brand universe, probably aimed at modernising its somewhat outdated image, at gaining new relevance in an ever more art-driven world (Chevalier/Mazzalovo, 2012, p. 209) and at expanding its reach by tapping into a younger and more trend-conscious customer segment (Hamza, 2012).

(2) Hugo Boss Prize: Since 1996, the Hugo Boss Prize is awarded every other year by the independent German high fashion brand of the same name (founded in 1924), to an artist who has made an important contribution to the contemporary art scene. In addition to a monetary reward of US$100,000, the winner is given the opportunity to showcase his works in the context of a solo exhibition at the renowned Solomon R. Guggenheim Museum in New York. Administered by the latter's foundation and sponsored by *Hugo Boss* (Hugo Boss eMAG, 2013), the prize has succeeded, since its establishment, in becoming a prestigious reference within the international art world and is today broadly recognised for reliably short-listing a handpicked selection of the most influential contemporary artists (Glueck, 1998). The Hugo Boss Prize differs from competing art awards by the absence of any age-, gender-, nationality- or media-related restrictions and is awarded, by a jury that comprises leading curators, critics and collectors, exclusively on the basis of directly art-related criteria such as innovation and creativity (Hugo Boss eMAG, 2013). The pictures in figure 13 show a promotional poster announcing the Hugo Boss Prize 2012, the Danish-Vietnamese conceptual artist Danh Vo who was awarded the Hugo Boss Prize in 2012 as well as one of the artist's works that were exhibited in a solo show at the Guggenheim Museum during spring 2013.

While the Hugo Boss Prize appears at first sight to benefit especially the honoured artist, *Hugo Boss* profits at least as much from the public attention that the prize provokes as the recipient himself. Put differently, because the high-profile awards ceremony creates, for comparatively little money and on a both recurrent and sustained basis, valuable buzz for the brand *Hugo Boss*, the Hugo Boss Prize can be regarded as an effective image enhancement tool. Also, the brand most likely generates additional social legitimisation through its voluntary commitment to the arts. The positive effect on *Hugo Boss*' public image can be judged even greater given that the collaborating parties target similar clienteles: Both *Hugo Boss* and the Guggenheim Museum cater to affluent, well-educated and highly cultured individuals (Glueck, 1998; Hugo Boss Group, 2013).

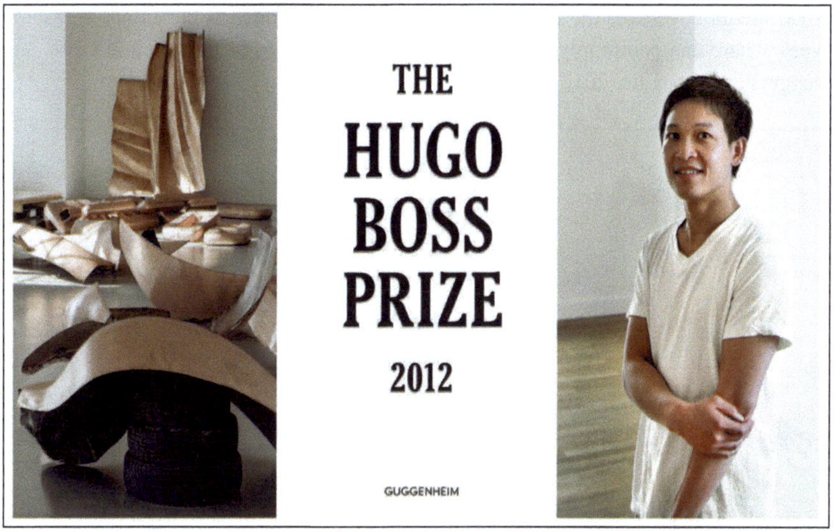

Figure 13: Impressions of the Hugo Boss Prize 2012
(Source: Guggenheim, 2013; Mousse Magazine, 2011).

(3) Margot Bowman's "Art Attack" on *Rupert Sanderson*: In 2012, the British luxury shoe manufacturer *Rupert Sanderson* joined forces with the illustrator Margot Bowman in the context of an experimental project that involved the temporary conversion of the brand's website into an "artistic hub" (Karmali, 2011). During the month-long collaboration, which was referred to by the independent young brand as "Art Attack", Bowman was given completely free hands to incorporate her creative language within the brand's online universe (Rupert Sanderson, 2012). More precisely, in order to endorse *Rupert Sanderson*'s latest collection in style, the illustrator was asked to reinvent the brand's launch campaign by transitorily changing the outer appearance of the website and transforming selected sections into dedicated spaces of personal creative expression and direct interaction with the consumer (Karmali, 2011). The pictures in figure 14 show some of the shoe-related artworks that Bowman created for *Rupert Sanderson*, a promotional flyer that was meant to communicate the unprecedented initiative to the press as well as the artist herself.

Albeit being publicly labelled as an unconventional project that would have only been implemented out of sympathy that the designer Sanderson shows for Bowman's creative vision, and would thus not have aimed at fulfilling any higher-ranking objective, the "Art Attack" was reportedly meant to inspire the brand a fresher image. Accordingly, in order to fully exploit the potential of this collaboration to generate broad media coverage, the project was scheduled in parallel to the London Fashion Week where one commonly encounters the highest density of fashion journalists and bloggers in town (Elle, 2012).

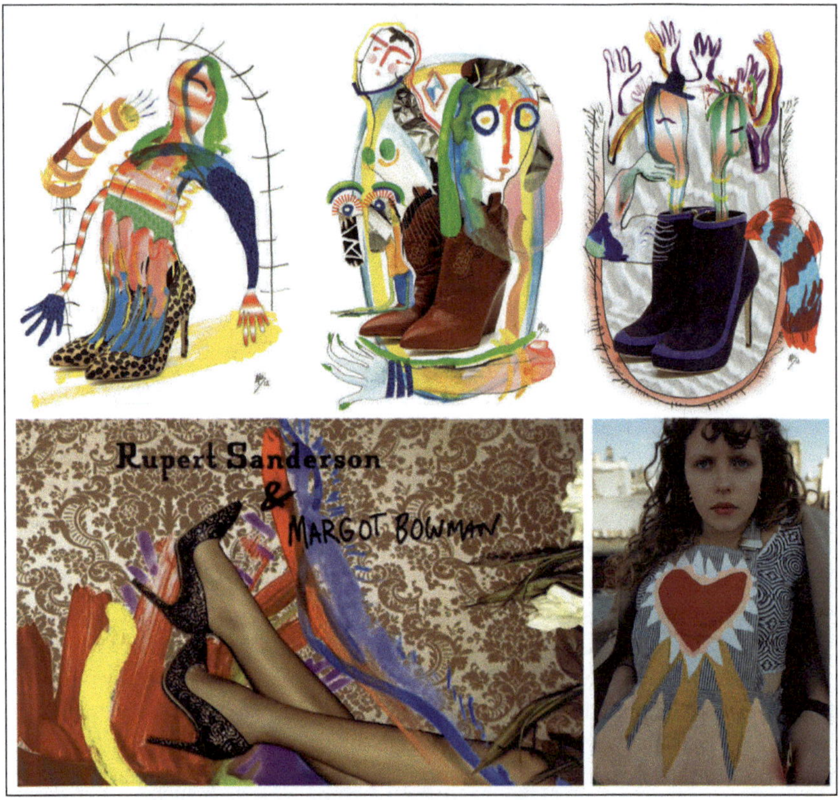

Figure 14: Impressions of Margot Bowman's Art Attack on *Rupert Sanderson* (Source: Davidson, 2012; Elle, 2012).

E. Closing remarks

1. Evaluation and limitations of the typological study

Since existing literature concepts have so far largely confined the phenomenon of LBACs to the theoretical proximity between the idea of luxury and that of art, the myriad, empirically observable forms of collaboration between luxury brands and the arts have remained virtually unexplored to date. By deriving distinct types of LBACs, this thesis intended to demonstrate the multifaceted nature of LBACs and to generate first scientific insights into the dominating collaborative patterns between luxury brands and the arts.

As regards the evaluation of the chosen research design, it can be stated that the typological approach, due to its both **explorative** and "**structure-seeking**" quality (Aaker et al., 2011, p. 502), is highly suitable to initially investigate fairly uncharted and disparate fields of inquiry, as was the case with LBACs. Accordingly, the descriptive cluster analysis ideally serves as the starting point for subsequent, more explicatory and/or normative research initiatives. Also, because the cluster analysis is typically performed on the basis of large quantitative data sets, it is supposed to provide quite **representative results** (Tan/Steinbach/Kumar, 2005, p. 487ff.). In this regard, the sample size of 136 real cases of LBACs can be considered as being sufficiently large in order to produce generalisable conclusions regarding the collaborative forms between luxury brands and the arts.

The typological study generated three fundamental insights into the concept of LBACs. First, it supports the initial assumption that LBACs constitute a both popular and **recurrent approach** in the international luxury goods industry since around 16% of all analysed luxury brands are currently, or have previously been using LBACs. The latter's actual relevance can most likely be estimated even higher because the internet-based approach to selecting LBACs has possibly not identified all LBACs that have ever been initiated by luxury brands. It can thus be concluded that, in the case of luxury brands, the practice of integrating art into branding and marketing activities is – in contrast to other industries –not a negligible niche strategy, but an **important, both tactical and strategic brand management tool**. Secondly, the empirical study proves that LBACs do not represent a uniform strategy, but become manifest in three distinct types: '**Arty Limited Edition**', '**Philanthropic LBAC**' and '**Experimental LBAC**'. The soundness of the cluster solution is supported by both statistical and practical considerations. On the one hand, given that the chi-square test produced very, respectively highly significant results for eight out of the selected nine attributes, the latter can be qualified as being effective in distinguishing different forms of LBACs. On the other hand, the derived LBAC-types reflect the reasons why luxury brands would seek proximity to the arts (cf. C.2.1.1-2.1.4): The re-emphasis of exclusivity and scarcity for the 'Arty Limited Edition', the attainment of social legitimisation and recognition for the 'Philanthropic LBAC' and the generation of creativity, newness and additional brand content for the 'Experimental LBAC'. Thirdly, the quantitative study offers valuable clues to a potential **conceptualisation of LBACs.** Because the attributes do not only describe the LBAC-types in their underlying characteristics, but also give first hints about their strategic orientation and operational implementation, the developed typology provides managers of luxury brands with initial guidance on the realisation of LBACs. Managers are thus not only offered **three distinct options** for the implementation of LBACs, but can also refer to the characteristic values of the three types as a **sort of preliminary checklist** for the execution of LBACs. The prototypical cases may serve in this regard as a further orientation and potentially even as **best practice examples.**

Yet, the typological approach also gives rise to certain limitations. First, given that cluster analyses often form the point of departure for exploring fairly under-researched topics, they regularly lack "an underlying theoretical rationale". As a result, the derived clusters may "not reflect any real conditions, but instead may simply be statistical artifacts that capitalize on random numerical variation". Secondly, because cluster analyses do not offer a test statistic (such as the F-statistic) (Ketchen/Shook, 1996, p. 442), but refer to rather simple statistical procedures (Aaker et al., 2011, p. 502), there is usually no reliable support for the generated results. Thirdly, due to the strong influence that the individual researcher exerts on the final cluster solution, the latter is to a certain extent subjectively biased and hence rather the effect of a "structure-imposing" operation (Aaker et al., 2011, p. 502). Lastly, the fuzziness of the typological approach does not permit to draw any firm conclusion on what attribute represented the decisive factor for the cluster formation.

In light of the weaknesses of the typological approach, future research projects might further test the robustness of the derived 3-cluster solution by:

- Letting (at least) two independent coders re-perform the cluster analysis;
- Simultaneously considering all 23 attributes within one cluster analysis;
- Conducting one of the partitioning clustering methods in order to check whether the initial assignment of the empirical cases of LBACs to the three clusters could possibly be further optimised (Backhaus et al., 2011, p. 418ff.);

- Performing a discriminant analysis in order to verify whether the identified combinations of characteristic values effectively differentiate between the three known LBAC-types (Aaker et al., 2011, p. 469ff.).

Yet, as the typology is only a first step towards a deeper understanding of LBACs, future research might, once the robustness of the 3-cluster solution is substantiated, go beyond the descriptive level and explore the management, effect and internal levels of LBACs.

(1) Management level: In order to help brand managers implement LBACs, key success factors for the three LBAC-types could be derived by differentiating between primary dimensions of success (e.g. internal vs. external or economic vs. non-economic goals), indicators of success (e.g. innovation output, profit, brand equity or corporate reputation) and drivers of success (e.g. fit, awareness of the artist, communicative support of the LBAC or project budget). The derived model could subsequently be tested for its practical relevance both qualitatively (e.g. case studies and action research) and quantitatively (e.g. laboratory experiments with consumers and surveys of luxury brand managers).

(2) Effect level: The impact of LBACs on the consumer's perception of, and attitude towards luxury brands could be discovered quantitatively through laboratory experiments and in comparison with related branding initiatives (e.g. celebrity endorsement or CRM).

(3) Internal level: While this thesis has taken an external view on LBACs, future research may adopt the opposite perspective by analysing the internal effects of LBACs on the brand identity, corporate culture, processes and employees via longitudinal case studies (Yin, 2009, p. 49). Moreover, while this thesis has so far assumed that LBACs can be treated as an explicit strategy that is deliberately pursued by luxury brands, some authors assert that LBACs are rather the accidental result of personal acquaintances and inclinations of the luxury brand's creative director or CEO (e.g. Arts & Business, 2012, p. 12; Tungate, 2009, p. 109ff.). Through one-to-one interviews and multiple case studies, future research might thus discover the context in which LBACs are actually entered into in reality. To this effect, it would be interesting to examine what the departure of an art-loving creative director such as Marc Jacobs (Garratt, 2012; Gropp, 2013) would imply for the luxury brand's collaborative behaviour vis-à-vis the arts in terms of frequency of occurrence, artistic know-how, contacts and relational capabilities. In this regard, it could be eventually probed whether common management rules are conducive to the success of LBACs or rather run contrary to the creative director's strong intuition and artistic mindset.

2. Outlook

Although some authors are convinced that LBACs will continue to flourish in the near future (e.g. Chevalier/Mazzalovo, 2012, p. 211; Lieblich, 2013), the reasons they cite rather suggest that the practice of LBACs runs the risk of losing its particular allure in the medium to longer term (Burns, 2012). While it is true that the art system, due to its **ongoing commercialisation** (Graw, 2008), has recently become both more comprehensible and accessible to the masses (Michau, 2009), it cannot be automatically concluded that the enlarged scope of art in today's society (Petersen, 2008) would provide luxury brands with an additional incentive to keep seeking proximity to the arts in the future as well. The **concomitant demystification of art** (Chevalier/Mazzalovo, 2012, p. 212; similar: Farago, 2012) rather runs contrary to the underlying rationale of LBACs. That is to say, while it was especially the transcendent character, non-material quality, unbound creativity and difficult-to-access inherent laws of the arts that have initially motivated luxury brands to join forces with them (Kapferer/Bastien, 2012, p. 32ff.), the more the art world is rooted in the real economy and becomes a **constituent part of a primarily hedonistic and consumption-oriented lifestyle** (Burns, 2012), the more it jeopardises its unique appeal to, and capacity to bestow upon luxury brands both cultural and social legitimisation (Petersen, 2008). On the other hand, the **increased trivialisation of art** prevents the latter from continuing performing its strong social demarcation function that was initially meant to serve as an elitist multiplier of the exclusive positioning of the luxury brand and effective remedy for the current up- and down-trading tendencies (Michau, 2009).

Also, while the fact that ever more luxury brands decide to join forces with the arts today highlights indeed the current popularity of LBACs, it does not necessarily hint at the lasting appeal of these collaborations. Rather, the more luxury brands team up with the arts, the more likely it is that a certain **wear-out effect** sets in, in the course of which LBACs are no longer perceived as disruptive branding initiatives, but rather as a regular and hence predictable element of the luxury brand's universe[73]. The empirical finding that luxury brands tend to team up time and again with the same

73 Albeit being oftentimes cited as best practice example (Maxwell, 2011), the regular collaborations between *Louis Vuitton* and the contemporary art world do no longer produce a surprise effect, but are today rather perceived as an integral part of the brand's distinct positioning (Petersen, 2008).

artists and art institutions further fuels this supposed wear-out effect (cf. D.2.2.2; appendix n 9) and may even suggest that it is less the artist's particular creative language or the art institution's unique profile that decides on the formation of LBACs, but rather a certain commercial and/or entrepreneurial mindset that the artist respectively art institution is commonly known for.

Moreover, while it is true that LBACs usually produce a win-win situation for their constituent parties (Boche, 2010; Maxwell, 2011; Swengley, 2011) and that it can thus be assumed that many other luxury brands will "quickly join […] the bandwagon" (Michau, 2009), the possibly **corruptive effect of luxury brands** on the originally virginal artistic mindset could sustainably derogate the appeal of these collaborations (Burns, 2012). To give but one example, when Marc Jacobs first approached Takashi Murakami in 2002 with the objective of jointly launching an arty limited edition bag, Murakami merely represented an unknown local artist who had not attracted any international attention by then. Yet, after the collaboration turned out to be a huge commercial success (Radon, 2012, p. 108), Murakami fully integrated the work he did for *Louis Vuitton* into his own artistic oeuvre and has, ever since, established himself as a highly publicised artist and savvy entrepreneur (Saltz, 2007). Since artists "are [thus] often in fact created by those who support their work" (Klanten/Ehmann/Sinofzik, 2012, p. 9), there is reason to suspect that, in the case of LBACs, the artist is less an artist in the proper sense of the word, but rather a "**commissioned creative**". The arts' dependence on the luxury brand would eventually even lead to a situation where they are "at no time […] allowed to express themselves freely. Their ideas are [rather] spread out, laid out and placed in PowerPoint displays; validated at multiple levels over many different presentations" (Michau, 2009).

Against this backdrop, it becomes understandable that the increased recourse to art by especially larger luxury labels has partially been sparking **harsh criticism**. While artists that decide to collaborate with luxury brands in order to generate public visibility, additional funds and a "dash of myth" (Boche, 2010) are usually blamed for betraying their artistic vocation by "selling their soul to the [capitalist] devil" (Michau, 2009), luxury brands are accused of **reviving a sort of cultural colonialism** (Maxwell, 2011) and equated with "gatekeepers" that have the power to make the difference between success and failure of upcoming talents within the art world (Kapferer/Bastien, 2012, p. 107). LBACs would accordingly turn art into a **vicarious agent of the luxury goods industry** and deprive art of its characteristic independence and eminent position in society.

Yet, it would be wrong to finally conclude that, in light of the above, the practice of LBACs would have no future prospects of success. Rather, in order to confront these risks, it appears vital to pay close attention to the diligent implementation of LBACs. To this effect, special emphasis should be laid on the four following aspects. First, luxury brands must dare to select an artistic counterpart that notably embodies **creative authenticity and (financial) independence** given that "the most successful collaborations are those in which artists do not significantly change their strategies, staying true to the essence of their work" (Letwin, 2013). Secondly and as a result of the latter fact, luxury brands should avoid subjecting their artistic counterpart to overly strict, brand- and/or product-related constraints, but rather commit themselves to the **promotion of artistic innovations and experiments** (Arnault, 2001, p. 119). Thirdly, they need to prevent their commercial concerns from prevailing too obviously over the artistic focus of the LBAC (Arnault, 2001, p. 118) because "once an alliance looks mercenary, it ceases to work" (Maxwell, 2011). Lastly, in order to counter the impending wear-out effect, luxury brands should be willing to truly engage with their artistic counterpart and to **further explore unconventional opportunities for collaboration** (Arnault, 2001, p. 120) – since "if used with integrity, [LBACs] can reinforce a luxury brand's currency and attraction" (Maxwell, 2011).

List of references

Aaker, D. A./Kumar, V./Day, G. S./Leone, R. P. (2011), Marketing research, 10th edition, Hoboken/New Jersey.

Adlwarth, W. (1983), Formen und Bestimmungsgründe prestigegeleiteten Konsumverhaltens. Eine verhaltenstheoretisch-empirische Analyse, Munich.

Amed, I. (2013), Why creative directors matter more than ever, http://www.businessoffashion.com/2013/06/why-creative-directors-matter-more-than-ever.html (accessed the 12th June 2013).

American Express (2006), 21st Centurion Living. Die Zukunft des Luxus unseres Jahrhunderts, http://www.weise-kommunikation.de/files/ebook_21_clr.pdf (accessed the 26th June 2013).

Arnault, B. (2001), in: Wetlaufer, S. (2001), The perfect paradox of star brands. An interview with Bernard Arnault of LVMH, in: Harvard Business Review, Vol. 79, No. 9, pp. 116-123.

Arthur, W. B. (1994), Inductive reasoning and bounded rationality, in: American Economic Review, Vol. 84, No. 2, pp. 406-411.

Arts & Business (2012), Creative liaisons. The luxury industry and the arts, http://www.artsandbusinessni.org.uk/documents/2012-05-15-12-15-14-25-09Jul_REI_Culture%20and%20the%20luxury%20sector.pdf (accessed the 27th February 2013).

Austin, R./Devin, L. (2003), Artful making. What managers need to know about how artists work, Upper Saddle River.

Bacher, J. (1996), Clusteranalyse. Anwendungsorientierte Einführung, 2nd edition, Munich/Vienna.

Bacher, J./Pöge, A./Wenzig, K. (2010), Clusteranalyse. Anwendungsorientierte Einführung in Klassifikationsverfahren, 3rd edition, Munich.

Backhaus, K./Erichson, B./Plinke, W./Weiber, R. (2011), Multivariate Analysemethoden. Eine anwendungsorientierte Einführung, 13th edition, Berlin/ Heidelberg.

Bailey, K. D. (1994), Typologies and taxonomies. An introduction to classification techniques, Thousand Oaks.

Barron, N. (2012), Where fashion meets art. The current trend for designer/artist collaborations, http://fashion.telegraph.co.uk/news-features/TMG9406097/Where-fashion-meets-art-the-current-trend-for-designerartist-collaborations.html (accessed the 1st July 2013).

Baumgarth, C. (2003), Wirkungen des Co-Brandings. Erkenntnisse durch Mastertechnikpluralismus, Wiesbaden.

Baumgarth, C. (2008), Markenpolitik. Markenwirkungen – Markenführung – Markencontrolling, 3rd edition, Wiesbaden.

Baumgarth, C./Bernecker, M. (1999), Marketingforschung, Munich.

Baumgarth, C./Lohrisch, N./Kaluza, M. (2012), Art meets business. Kann Kunst nicht auch Impulsgeber für Management sein? (unpublished research proposal).

Baumgarth, C./Lohrisch, N./Kaluza, M. (2013), Arts push business. Welchen Nutzen hat Kunst für Unternehmen tatsächlich? (submitted to, and accepted by Fachverband Kulturmanagement).

Bearden, W. O./Etzel, M. J. (1982), Reference group influence on product and brand purchase decisions, in: Journal of Consumer Research, Vol. 9, No. 2, pp. 183-194.

Becker, J. (1996), Konzeptionelle Grundfragen der Positionierung, in: Tomczak, T./ Rudolph, T./Roosdorp, A. (1996, Eds), Positionierung. Kernentscheidung des Marketing, St. Gallen, pp. 12-23.

Bergs, S. (1981), Optimalität bei Cluster-Analysen. Experimente zur Bewertung numerischer Klassifikationsverfahren, Munich.

Berlyne, D. E. (1974), Studies in the new experimental aesthetics. Steps toward an objective psychology of aesthetic appreciation, Washington DC.

Berndt, R. (2005), Marketingstrategie und Marketingpolitik, 4th edition, Berlin/ Heidelberg.

Betz, G./Hitzler, R./Pfadenhauer, M. (2011, Eds), Urbane Events, Wiesbaden.

Bezuglov, D. (2013), Outsider art. The writing is on the wall for street artist Timofei Radya, http://calvertjournal.com/articles/show/562/outsider-art-yekaterinburg-street-artist-timofei-radya (accessed the 16th July 2013).

Bhuyan, R. (2012), Different forms of art, http://www.buzzle.com/articles/different-forms-of-art.html (accessed the 19th March 2013).

Biehl-Missal, B. (2011), Wirtschaftsästhetik. Wie Unternehmen die Kunst als Inspiration und Werkzeug nutzen, Wiesbaden.

Binlot, A. (2012), Marc Jacobs recruits Yayoi Kusama for latest Louis Vuitton collaboration, http://www.artinfo.com/news/story/755503/marc-jacobs-recruits-yayoi-kusama-for-latest-louis-vuitton-collaboration (accessed the 27th December 2012).

Bivainiene, L. (2010), Brand life cycle. Theoretical discourses, in: Economics & Management, Vol. 15, pp. 408-414.

Boche, G. (2010), The artketing age of luxury, http://fblog.futurebrand.com/the-artketing-age-of-luxury/ (accessed the 23rd December 2012).

Bode, O. F. (2011), Kulturmanagement, in: Lewinski-Reuter, V./Lüddemann, S. (2011, Eds), Glossar Kulturmanagement, Wiesbaden, pp. 160-174.

Bourdieu, P. (1979), La distinction. Critique sociale du jugement, Paris.

Bourdieu, P./Darbel, A. (1991), The love of art. European art museums and their public, Cambridge.

Braun, M. (1997), Becoming an institutional brand. A long-term strategy for luxury goods, Bamberg.

Bronder, C. (1993), Kooperationsmanagement. Unternehmensdynamik durch Strategische Allianzen, Frankfurt on the Main.

Bruce, M./Kratz, C. (2007), Competitive marketing strategies of luxury fashion companies, in: Hines, T./Bruce, M. (2007, Eds), Fashion marketing. Contemporary issues, 2nd edition, Oxford, pp. 130-150.

Bruhn, M. (2004), Begriffsabgrenzungen und Erscheinungsformen von Marken, in: Bruhn, M. (2004, Ed.), Handbuch Markenführung. Kompendium zum erfolgreichen Markenmanagement. Strategien – Instrumente – Erfahrungen, 2nd edition, Wiesbaden, pp. 3-49.

Bruhn, M. (2010), Sponsoring. Systematische Planung und integrativer Einsatz, 5th edition, Wiesbaden.

Burmann, C./Meffert, H. (2005), Theoretisches Grundkonzept der identitätsorientierten Markenführung, in: Meffert, H./Burmann, C./Koers, M. (2005, Eds), Markenmanagement. Identitätsorientierte Markenführung und praktische Umsetzung, 2nd edition, Wiesbaden, pp. 37-72.

Burmann, C./Meffert, H./Koers, M. (2005), Stellenwert und Gegenstand des Markenmanagements, in: Meffert, H./Burmann, C./Koers, M. (2005, Eds), Markenmanagement. Identitätsorientierte Markenführung und praktische Umsetzung, 2nd edition, Wiesbaden, pp. 3-17.

Burns, C. (2012), Can their love last forever?, http://www.theartnewspaper.com/articles/Can-their-love-last-forever/28210 (accessed the 29th June 2013).

Büschken, J./von Thaden, C. (2000), Clusteranalyse, in: Herrmann, A./Homburg, C. (2000, Eds), Marktforschung. Methoden – Anwendungen – Praxisbeispiele, 2nd edition, Wiesbaden, pp. 337-380.

Büttner, M./Huber, F./Regier, S./Vollhardt, K. (2006), Phänomen Luxusmarke. Identitätsstiftende Effekte und Determinanten der Markenloyalität, Wiesbaden.

BVerfGE 30, 173/188, Mephisto, http://www.servat.unibe.ch/dfr/bv030173.html (accessed the 18th July 2013).

BVerfGE 67, 213/225, Anachronistischer Zug, http://www.servat.unibe.ch/dfr/bv067213.html#Opinion (accessed the 18th July 2013).

BVerfGE 67, 213/226, Anachronistischer Zug, http://www.servat.unibe.ch/dfr/bv067213.html (accessed the 18th July 2013).

Calinski, T./Harabasz, J. (1974), A dendrite method for cluster analysis, in: Communications in Statistics, Vol. 3, No. 1, pp. 1-27.

Cartner-Morley, J. (2012), Yves Saint Laurent to be renamed by creative director Hedi Slimane, http://www.guardian.co.uk/fashion/2012/jun/21/yves-saint-laurent-renamed (accessed the 2nd May 2013).

Catry, B. (2003), The great pretenders. The magic of luxury goods, in: Business Strategy Review, Vol. 14, No. 3, pp. 10-17.

Causse Gantier (2012), http://blog.causse-gantier.fr/articles/causse-arty/ (accessed the 19th May 2013).

Chanel Mobile Art Pavilion (2013), http://www.chanel-mobileart.com/?lang=en_eu (accessed the 30th April 2013).

Chayka, K. (2012), How the art world's lingo of exclusivity took root, branched out, and then rotted from within, http://www.artinfo.com/news/story/817400/how-the-art-worlds-lingo-of-exclusivity-took-root-branched-out-and-then-rotted-from-within (accessed the 29th March 2013).

Chevalier, M./Mazzalovo, G. (2012), Luxury brand management. A world of privilege, 2nd edition, Hoboken/New Jersey.

Chiu, E. (2011), KAWS x Hennessy V.S. Cognac limited edition bottle, http://hypebeast.com/2011/7/kaws-x-hennessy-v-s-cognac-limited-edition-bottle?_locale=en (accessed the 30th April 2013).

Círculo Fortuny (2013), http://www.circulofortuny.com/ (accessed the 2nd May 2013).

Comité Colbert (2013), http://www.comitecolbert.com/ (accessed the 13th February 2013).

Cooper, N. (2012), Emerging luxury strategies. Insights from BrandZ, http://www.millwardbrown.com/Libraries/MB_Articles_Downloads/MillwardBrown_EmergingLuxury_BrandZstrategies.sflb.ashx (accessed the 22nd July 2013).

Cothey, A. L. (1990), The nature of art, London/New York.

Dalloz, X. (2011), Rapport ATAWAD, http://www.cjd-paris.fr/leblog/wp-content/uploads/2011/07/Rapport-ATAWAD-de-Mai-2011.pdf (accessed the 23rd March 2013).

Dams, V./Dams, C. M. (2008), Code Rouge. Gesetze des Erfolges für Events und Live-Marketing, Frankfurt on the Main.

Danto, A. (1964), The artworld, in: The Journal of Philosophy, Vol. 61, No. 19, pp. 571-584.

Darso, L. (2004), Artful creation. Learning tales of arts-in-business, Copenhagen.

Davidson, J. (2012), Margot Bowman for Kiehl's. Hot British talent celebrates Earth Day with New York-based skincare brand, http://www.weheart.co.uk/2012/03/02/margot-bowman-for-kiehls/ (accessed the 7th June 2013).

De Barnier, V./Rodina, I./Valette-Florence, P. (2006), Which luxury perceptions affect most consumer purchase behavior? A cross cultural exploratory study in France, the United Kingdom and Russia, in: Proceedings des Congrés Paris-Venise des Tendences Marketing, Paris.

Deimer, R. (1986), Unscharfe Clusteranalysemethoden. Eine problemorientierte Darstellung zur unscharfen Klassifikation gemischter Daten, Idstein.

Designboom (2011), Zaha Hadid. Chanel Mobile Art Pavilion Paris, http://www.designboom.com/architecture/zaha-hadid-chanel-mobile-art-pavilion-paris/ (accessed the 30th April 2013).

De Villiers, M. (2011), Hermès Singapore store tagged by Kongo, http://travel.cnn.com/singapore/shop/vandalized-hermes-singapore-store-tagged-kongo-816767 (accessed the 7th June 2013).

Dewey, J. (1958), Art as experience. The quest for certainty, individualism, old and new philosophy and civilization, 15th edition, New York.

Dickie, G. (1974), Art and the aesthetic. An institutional analysis, Ithaca/London.

Dickie, G. (1984), The art circle, New York.

Dion, D./Arnould, E. (2011), Retail luxury strategy. Assembling charisma through art and magic, in: Journal of Retailing, Vol. 87, No. 4, pp. 502-520.

Doc News (2013), The art of collaboration by Peter Lindbergh, http://www.docnews.fr/actualites/marque,the-art-collaboration-peter-lindbergh,30,15974.html (accessed the 19th May 2013).

Dom Pérignon (2013), http://www.domperignon.com/de/image/home-power-of-creation/ (accessed the 19th May 2013).

Drucker, P. F. (1974), Management. Tasks – responsibilities – practices, New York.

Dubois, B./Laurent, G./Czellar, S. (2001), Consumer rapport to luxury. Analyzing complex and ambivalent attitudes, http://www.hec.fr/var/fre/storage/original/application/5ecca063454eb4ef8227d08506a8673b.pdf (accessed the 4th February 2013).

Dubois, B./Paternault, C. (1995), Observations: Understanding the world of international luxury brands. The "dream formula", in: Journal of Advertising Research, Vol. 35, No. 4, pp. 69-76.

Eckes, T. (1991), Psychologie der Begriffe. Strukturen des Wissens und Prozesse der Kategorisierung, Göttingen/Toronto/Zurich.

Elite Choice (2011), Hermès-Kongo collaboration results in explosively colourful scarves, http://elitechoice.org/2011/08/30/hermes-kongo-collaboration-results-in-explosively-colorful-scarves/ (accessed the 7th June 2013).

Elle (2012), Under art attack, http://www.elle.de/fashion-fashion-news-mode-news-under-art-attack-105246.html (accessed the 7th June 2013).

Elliott, S. (2012), Hennessy goes 'wild' for the pursuit of achievement, http://www.nytimes.com/2012/03/19/business/media/hennessy-goes-wild-for-the-pursuit-of-achievement-campaign-spotlight.html?pagewanted=all&_r=0 (accessed the 30th April 2013).

Emundts, R. (2003), Kunst- und Kulturförderung, Berlin.

Ernst, D./French, T. D. (1996), Coffee and one way to Boston, in: The McKinsey Quarterly, No. 1, pp. 165-175.

Esaak, S. (2011a), What is visual art?, http://www.artlex.com/ (accessed the 18th March 2013).

Esaak, S. (2011b), Performance art. Art history 101 basics, http://www.artlex.com/ (accessed the 19th March 2013).

Esch, F.-R. (2001), Markenpositionierung als Grundlage der Markenführung, in: Esch, F.-R. (2001, Ed.), Moderne Markenführung. Grundlagen – Innovative Ansätze – Praktische Umsetzungen, 3rd edition, Wiesbaden, pp. 233-265.

Farago, J. (2012), Damien Hirst's transition from artist to luxury brand is complete, http://www.newrepublic.com/blog/plank/111155/hirsts-transition-artist-luxury-brand-complete# (accessed the 3rd July 2013).

Feldman, T. (1997), An introduction to digital media, London.

Figal, G. (2012), Kunst. Philosophische Abhandlungen, Tübingen.

Filicko, T./Lafferty, S. A. (1999), Defining the arts and cultural universe. Early lessons from the profiles project (paper presented at the 28th Annual Conference of the Association for Research on Nonprofit organizations and Voluntary Action).

Flamini, R. (2008), The art of luxury. The love affair between corporate philanthropists and contemporary creators, http://www.francemagazine.org/articles/issue87/article222.asp?issue_id=87&article_id=222 (accessed the 17th July 2013).

Flew, T. (2005), New media. An introduction, Oxford/New York.

Fog, K./Budtz, C./Yakaboylu, B. (2005), Storytelling. Branding in practice, Berlin.

Fondazione Altagamma (2013), http://www.altagamma.it/sezione1.php (accessed the 2nd May 2013).

Foulkes, N. (2009), Where art meets luxury design, http://www.thedailybeast.com/newsweek/2009/06/26/where-art-meets-luxury-design.html (accessed the 1st July 2013).

Freeland, C. (2003), Auch das ist Kunst. Eine Einführung in die Kunsttheorie, Zurich/Berlin.

Friedman, H. H./Friedman, L. (1979), Endorser effectiveness by product type, in: Journal of Advertising Research, Vol. 19, No. 5, pp. 63-71.

Friedman, H. H./Termini, S./Washington, R. (1976), The effectiveness of advertisement utilizing four types of endorsers, in: Journal of Advertising, Vol. 5, No. 3, pp. 22-24.

Friedrichs, J. (1990), Methoden empirischer Sozialforschung, 14th edition, Opladen.

Frisk, H./Karlsson, H. (2011), Time and interaction. Research through non-visual arts and media, in: Biggs, M./Karlsson, H. (2011, Eds), The Routledge Companion to research in the arts, Abingdon, pp. 277-292.

Fuchs, M. (2011), Kunst als kulturelle Praxis. Kunsttheorie und Ästhetik für Kulturpolitik und Pädagogik, http://www.bkj.de/fileadmin/user_upload/documents/theoriebildung_grundlagen/06_Fuchs_2011_Kunst_als_kulturelle_Praxis_Kunsttheorie_und_Aesthetik_fuer_Kulturpolitik_und_Paedagogik.pdf (accessed the 18th February 2013).

Funch, B. S. (1997), The psychology of art appreciation, Copenhagen.

Galbraith, J. R. (1998), Designing the networked organization. Leveraging size and competencies, in: Mohrman, S. A./Galbraith, J. R./Lawler, E. E. III. and Associates (1998, Eds), Tomorrow's organization. Crafting winning capabilities in a dynamic world, San Francisco, pp. 76-102.

Garratt, S. (2012), The dotty art of Yayoi Kusama comes to Louis Vuitton, http://www.telegraph.co.uk/culture/art/art-features/9378909/The-dotty-art-of-Yayoi-Kusama-comes-to-Louis-Vuitton.html (accessed the 27th December 2012).

Gaut, B. (2002), „Kunst" als Clusterbegriff, in: Bluhm, R./Schmücker, R. (2002, Eds), Kunst und Kunstbegriff. Der Streit um die Grundlagen der Ästhetik, Paderborn, pp. 140-165.

Gethmann-Siefert, A. (1995), Einführung in die Ästhetik, Munich.

GG Art. 5(3), Grundgesetz Artikel 5, http://dejure.org/gesetze/GG/5.html (accessed the 18th July 2013).

Glueck, G. (1998), Contemporary works intended to provoke, http://www.nytimes.com/1998/07/17/arts/art-review-contemporary-works-intended-to-provoke.html (accessed the 7th June 2013).

Goldenberg, D./Reed, P. (2008), What is a participatory practice?, http://fillip.ca/content/what-is-a-participatory-practice (accessed the 23rd March 2013).

Goodrow, G./Conzen, F./Salie, O. (2012, Eds), Corporate collections, Cologne.

Graw, I. (2008), Der große Preis. Kunst zwischen Markt und Celebrity, Cologne.

Green, Y. (2011), Is time really everything? Time-based artists, http://chicagoartmagazine.com/2011/01/is-time-really-everything-time-based-artists/ (accessed the 7th June 2013).

Gropp, R.-M. (2013), Über die Liaison von Kunst und Mode, http://www.faz.net/aktuell/gesellschaft/mode/zeitgeschehen-ueber-die-liaison-von-kunst-und-mode-12114399.html (accessed the 8th July 2013).

Grugel-Pannier, D. (1996), Luxus. Eine begriffs- und ideengeschichtliche Untersuchung unter besonderer Berücksichtigung von Bernard Mandeville, Frankfurt on the Main/New York.

Guggenheim (2013), http://www.guggenheim.org/guggenheim-foundation/annual-reports/category/4-sample-pages (accessed the 7th June 2013).

Hagestedt, J. (2008), Über den Unterschied zwischen „ernster“ und „Unterhaltungsmusik“, in: Merkur, No. 707, pp. 294-306.

Hagtvedt, H./Patrick, V. M. (2008), Art infusion. The influence of visual art on the perception and evaluation of consumer products, in: Journal of Marketing Research, Vol. 45, No. 3, pp. 379-389.

Hair, J. F./Wolfinbarger Celsi, M./Money, A. H./Samouel, P./Page, M. J. (2011), Essentials of business research methods, 2nd edition, Armonk/London.

Hamza, S. (2012), Hermès v. Kongo, http://thebucketjournal.com/hermes-v-kongo/ (accessed the 7th June 2012).

Hauskeller, M. (2000), Was ist Kunst? Positionen der Ästhetik von Platon bis Danto, 5th edition, Munich.

Hausmann, A. (2011), Kunst- und Kulturmanagement. Kompaktwissen für Studium und Praxis, Wiesbaden.

Heine, K. (2011), The concept of luxury brands, http://www.conceptofluxurybrands.com/content/20110907_Heine_TheConceptofLuxuryBrands.pdf (accessed the 1st March 2013).

Heit, E. (2007), What is induction and why study it?, in: Feeney, A./Heit, E. (2007, Eds), Inductive reasoning. Experimental, developmental, and computational approaches, Cambridge, pp. 1-24.

Hennessy (2013), http://www.hennessy.com/us/news/tagging-the-hennessy-bottle-with-futura/ (accessed the 30th April 2013).

Herbrand, N. O. (2008, Ed.), Schauplätze dreidimensionaler Markeninszenierung. Innovative Strategien und Erfolgsmodelle erlebnisorientierter Begegnungskommunikation. Brand Parks – Museen – Flagship Stores – Messen – Events – Roadshows, Stuttgart.

Hill, A. (1976, Ed.), DuMont’s Bild-Lexikon der Kunst. Künstler, Stile, Techniken. Von der Steinzeit bis zur Gegenwart, Cologne.

Holl, A. (1999), Empirische Wirtschaftsinformatik und Erkenntnistheorie, in: Becker, J./König, W./Schütte, R./Wendt, O./Zelewski, S. (1999, Eds), Wirtschaftsinformatik und Wissenschaftstheorie. Bestandsaufnahme und Perspektiven, Wiesbaden, pp. 163-207.

Holzberg, M. (2009), Erfolgsfaktoren sektorübergreifender Kooperationen, Wiesbaden.

Horizont (2011), Deutscher Medienkongress. Abgesang auf die 360-Grad-Kommunikation, http://www.horizont.net/aktuell/marketing/pages/protected/Deutscher-Medienkongress-Abgesang-auf-die-360-Grad-Kommunikation_97488.html (accessed the 1st May 2013).

Huettl, V./Gierl, H. (2012), Visual art in advertising. The effects of utilitarian vs. hedonic product positioning and price information, in: Marketing Letters: A Journal of Research in Marketing, Vol. 23, No. 3, pp. 893-904.

Hugill, A. (2012), Divine coalescence. A one-time video projection curated by Leo Kuelbs for Dom Pérignon, http://www.berlinartlink.com/2012/06/01/divine-coalescence-by-leo-kuelbs-for-dom-perignon/ (accessed the 25th April 2013).

Hugo Boss eMAG (2013), http://www.hugoboss.com/de/en/emag/artsSponsorship/hbPrize2012.php (accessed the 7thJune 2013).

Hugo Boss Group (2013), http://group.hugoboss.com/en/corporate_profile.htm (accessed the 7th June 2013)

Iacobucci, D./Churchill, G. A., (2010), Marketing research. Methodological foundations, 10th edition, Mason.

Interbrand (2008a), The leading luxury brands 2008, http://www.interbrand.com/Libraries/Branding_Studies/The_Leading_Luxury_Brands_2008.sflb.ashx (accessed the 7th February 2013).

Interbrand (2008b), Interbrand veröffentlicht Studie zu den wertvollsten Luxusmarken der Welt, http://www.interbrand.com/de/news-room/press-releases/Press-Release-DE-Luxury2008.aspx (accessed the 9th July 2013).

Interbrand (2012), Interbrand releases 13th annual best global brands report, http://www.interbrand.com/Libraries/Press_Release/BGB_Press_Release_FINAL.sflb.ashx (accessed the 16th March 2013).

Irvine, M. (2013), The institutional theory of art and the artworld, http://www9.georgetown.edu/faculty/irvinem/visualarts/institutional-theory-artworld.html (accessed the 22nd March 2013).

Jäckel, M./Kochhan, C. (2000), Notwendigkeit und Luxus. Ein Beitrag zur Geschichte des Konsums, in: Rosenkranz, D./Schneider, N. F. (2000, Eds), Konsum. Soziologische, ökonomische und psychologische Perspektiven, Opladen, pp. 73-93.

Joy, A./Sherry Jr., J. F. (2003), Speaking of art as embodied imagination. A multisensory approach to understanding aesthetic experience, in: Journal of Consumer Research, Vol. 30, No. 2, pp. 259-282.

Kaiser, A. (2013), Treffen der High-End-Marken. Darf's ein bisschen mehr sein?, http://www.faz.net/aktuell/gesellschaft/mode/treffen-der-high-end-marken-darf-s-ein-bisschen-mehr-sein-12126230.html (accessed the 30th March 2013).

Kamins, M. A. (1990), An investigation into the "match-up" hypothesis in celebrity advertising. When beauty may be only skin deep, in: Journal of Advertising, Vol. 19, No. 1, pp. 4-13.

Kapferer, J.-N. (2001), Luxusmarken, in: Esch, F.-R. (2001, Ed.), Moderne Markenführung. Grundlagen, innovative Ansätze, praktische Umsetzungen, 3rd edition, Wiesbaden, pp. 345-364.

Kapferer, J.-N. (2006), The two business cultures of luxury brands, in: Schroeder, J. E./Salzer-Mörling, M. (2006, Eds), Brand culture, Abingdon, pp. 67-76.

Kapferer, J.-N. (2012), The new strategic brand management. Advanced insights and strategic thinking, 5th edition, London.

Kapferer, J.-N./Bastien, V. (2009), The specificity of luxury management. Turning marketing upside down, in: Journal of Brand Management, Vol. 16, No. 5/6, pp. 311-322.

Kapferer, J.-N./Bastien, V. (2012), The luxury strategy. Break the rules of marketing to build luxury brands, 2nd edition, London.

Karmali, S. (2012), Rupert Sanderson's artistic project, http://www.vogue.co.uk/news/2012/09/11/rupert-sanderson-collaborates-with-margot-bowman-on-website-takeover (accessed the 7th June 2013).

Karpik, L. (2011), Mehr Wert. Die Ökonomie des Einzigartigen, Frankfurt on the Main.

Kelle, U./Kluge, S. (1999), Vom Einzelfall zum Typus. Fallvergleich und Fallkontrastierung in der qualitativen Sozialforschung, Opladen.

Keller, K. L. (1993), Conceptualizing, measuring, and managing customer-cased brand equity, in: Journal of Marketing, Vol. 57, No. 1, pp. 1-22.

Keller, K. L. (1998), Strategic brand management, Upper Saddle River.

Keller, K. L. (2001), Kundenorientierte Messung des Markenwerts, in: Esch, F.-R. (2001, Ed.), Moderne Markenführung. Grundlagen – Innovative Ansätze – Praktische Umsetzungen, 3rd edition, Wiesbaden, pp. 1059-1079.

Keller, K. L. (2003), Brand synthesis. The multidimensionality of brand knowledge, in: Journal of Consumer Research, Vol. 29, No. 4, pp. 595-600.

Keller, K. L./Apéria, T./Georgson, M. (2012), Strategic brand management. A European perspective, 2nd edition, Harlow.

Kennedy, D. (2010), Luxury brands. How to maneuver through this moment of austerity, http://www.interbrand.com/Libraries/Articles/52_IP_Luxury_Brands_pdf.sflb.ashx (accessed the 1st July 2013).

Kent, W. (2012), Hermès x Kongo scarf collection, http://elitedaily.com/featured/hermes-kongo-collection/ (accessed the 7th June 2013).

Ketchen, D. J./Shook, C. L. (1996), The application of cluster analysis in strategic management research. An analysis and critique, in: Strategic Management Journal, Vol. 17, No. 6, pp. 441-458.

Klanten, R./Ehmann, S./Sinofzik, A. (2012), Taken by surprise. Cutting-edge collaborations between designers, artists and brands, Berlin.

Kluge, S. (1999), Empirisch begründete Typenbildung. Zur Konstruktion von Typen und Typologien in der qualitativen Sozialforschung, Opladen.

K-MB New York (2013), http://www.k-mb.com/projects/mercedes-benz/the-avantgarde-diaries (accessed the 1st May 2013).

Knoblich, H. (1972), Die typologische Methode in der Betriebswirtschaftslehre, in: WiSt, Vol. 2, No. 4, pp. 141-147.

Kolb, H. L. (1988), Marketing für Zulieferunternehmen. Eine Untersuchung auf typologischer Grundlage, Frankfurt on the Main et al.

Kolesnikov-Jessop, S. (2010), The Chinese artist makes the brand, http://www.thedaily beast.com/newsweek/2010/08/13/chinese-artists-to-reimagine-top-luxury-brands.html (accessed the 28th December 2012).

Koller, M. (2007), Die Grenzen der Kunst. Luhmanns gelehrte Poesie, Wiesbaden.

Kosuth, J./Holzer, J./Ueltzhoeffer, R. (2012), Konzeptkunst, http://konzeptkunst4. wordpress.com/ (accessed the 19th March 2013).

Krieger, V. (2007), Was ist ein Künstler? Genie – Heilsbringer – Antikünstler. Eine Ideen- und Kunstgeschichte des Schöpferischen, Cologne.

Kromrey, H. (2009), Empirische Sozialforschung, 12th edition, Stuttgart.

Kuß, A. (2012), Marktforschung. Grundlage der Datenerhebung und Analyse, 4th edition, Wiesbaden.

La Tribune (2013), Hermès publie un chiffre d'affaire historique en 2012, http://www.latribune.fr/entreprises-finance/industrie/agroalimentaire-biens-de-con sommation-luxe/20130212trib000748258/hermes-publie-un-chiffre-d-affaires-hist orique-en-2012.html (accessed the 7th June 2013).

LaBoulbenne, X. (2005), Paris à la mode, http://www.artnet.com/magazineus/ reviews/laboulbenne/laboulbenne10-26-05.asp (accessed the 29th June 2013).

Lacoste (2013), http://www.lacoste.com/univers (accessed the 30th April 2013).

Lamb, R. (2012), Hennessy adds to wild rabbit campaign with Futura collaboration, http://www.luxurydaily.com/hennessy-adds-to-wild-rabbit-campaign-with-futura-collaboration/ (accessed the 30th April 2013).

Lasslop, I. (2003), Effektivität und Effizienz von Marketing-Events. Wirkungstheoretische Analyse und empirische Befunde, Wiesbaden.

Lasslop, I. (2005), Identitätsorientierte Führung von Luxusmarken, Meffert, H./ Burmann, C./Koers, M. (2005, Eds), Markenmanagement. Identitätsorientierte Markenführung und praktische Umsetzung, 2nd edition, Wiesbaden, pp. 469-494.

Lee, P. M. (2012), Forgetting the art world, Cambridge.

Lee, D. H./Park, C. W. (2007), Conceptualization and measurement of multidimensionality of integrated marketing communications, in: Journal of Advertising Research, Vol. 47, No. 3, pp. 222-236.

Leibenstein, H. (1950), Bandwagon, snob, and Veblen effects in the theory of consumers' demand, in: The Quarterly Journal of Economics, Vol. 64, No. 2, pp. 183-207.

Letwin, H. (2013), Art meets luxury branding. Bridge of sighs, http://montecristomagazine.com/magazine/summer-2013/art-meets-luxury-branding (accessed the 6th July 2013).

Levin, A. M./Davis, J. C./Levin, I. P. (1996), Theoretical and empirical linkages between consumers' responses to different branding strategies, in: Advances in Consumer Research, Vol. 23, No. 1, pp. 296-300.

LeWitt, S. (1967), Paragraphs on conceptual art, in: Artforum, Vol. 5, No. 10, pp. 79-83.

Lieblich, M. (2013), The changing face of collaborations in the luxury goods industry. Beyond the H&M collaboration phenomenon, http://blog.euromonitor.com/2013/04/the-changing-face-of-collaborations-in-the-luxury-goods-industry-beyond-the-hm-collaboration-phenome.html (accessed the 1st July 2013).

Lindemann, G./Boekhoff, H. (1970), Lexikon der Kunststile. Die verschiedenen Kunstrichtungen in typischen Beispielen aus Architektur, Plastik, Malerei, Mode und Kunsthandwerk, Reinbek.

Lorenzoni, G./Lipparini, A. (1999), The leveraging of interfirm relationships as a distinctive organizational capability. A longitudinal study, in: Strategic Management Journal, Vol. 20, No. 4, pp. 317-338.

Louis Vuitton Germany (2013), http://www.louisvuitton.de/front/#/deu_DE/search/MURAKAMI (accessed the 23rd January 2013).

Luhmann, N. (1995), Die Kunst der Gesellschaft, Frankfurt on the Main.

Luna, I. (2009, Ed.), Louis Vuitton. Art, fashion and architecture, New York.

LVMH Group (2013), http://www.lvmh.com/the-group/lvmh-group (accessed the 30th April 2013).

Maeland, A. (2011), Kongo for Hermès event recap, http://hypebeast.com/2011/10/kongo-for-hermes-event-recap (accessed the 7th of June 2013).

Mandeville, B. (1957), Die Bienenfabel oder private Laster als öffentliche Vorteile, Berlin.

Marandon, E. (2011), Warum Handtaschen keine Kunst sind, http://www.zeit.de/lebensart/mode/2011-11/Anselm-reyle-Dior-accessoires (accessed the 29th June 2013).

Marquart, C./Esch, H. G. (2004), Mercedes-Benz brand places. Architecture and interior design, Ludwigsburg.

Marraro, E. (2012), Wearable art. Designer/artist collaborations. From Jimmy Choo to Dior to Louis Vuitton, http://www.graziadaily.co.uk/fashion/archive/ 2012/10/25/jimmy-choo-1.htm (accessed the 1st July 2013).

Matlack, C. (2013), Kering, the new name of luxury brand PPR, means something else in Indonesian, http://www.businessweek.com/articles/2013-03-22/kering-the-new-name-of-luxury-brand-ppr-means-something-else-in-indonesian (accessed the 24th April 2013).

Matthews, R. J. (2002), Eine Verteidigung der traditionellen Ästhetik, in: Bluhm, R./ Schmücker, R. (2002, Eds), Kunst und Kunstbegriff. Der Streit um die Grundlagen der Ästhetik, Paderborn, pp. 95-117.

Maxwell, S. (2011), The art collaboration. Old masters to new blood, http://luxurysociety.com/articles/2011/11/the-art-collaboration-old-masters-to-new-blood (accessed the 23rd December 2012).

McDaniel, C. D./Gates, R. H. (2013), Marketing research, 9th edition, Hoboken/New Jersey.

McEvilley, T. (1997), in: Wallach, A. (1997), Art. Is it art? Is it good? And who says so?, http://www.nytimes.com/1997/10/12/arts/art-is-it-art-is-it-good-and-who-says-so.html?pagewanted=all&src=pm (accessed the 3rd April 2013).

McKay, C. (2012), Window installation by Rolf Sachs for De Beers, http://www.wallpaper.com/fashion/window-installation-by-rolf-sachs-for-de-beers/6196 (accessed the 29th June 2013).

McKinsey (1990, Ed.), The luxury industry. An asset for France, Paris.

Meffert, H./Burmann, C. (2005), Wandel in der Markenführung – vom instrumentellen zum identitätsorientierten Markenverständnis, in: Meffert, H./ Burmann, C./Koers, M. (2005, Eds), Markenmanagement. Identitätsorientierte Markenführung und praktische Umsetzung, 2nd edition, Wiesbaden, pp. 19-36.

Meffert, H./Lasslop, I. (2004), Luxusmarkenstrategie, in: Bruhn, M. (2004, Ed.), Handbuch Markenführung. Kompendium zum erfolgreichen Markenmanagement. Strategien – Instrumente – Erfahrungen, 2nd edition, Wiesbaden, pp. 927-947.

Meidl, C. N. (2009), Wissenschaftstheorien für SozialforscherInnen, Stuttgart.

Meissen (2013), Limitierte Meissener Kunstwerke als wunderschöne Wertanlage, http://www.meissen.com/de/limitierte-kunstwerke/meissen-als-wertanlage/ jahreseditionen (accessed the 20th of April 2013).

Meisterkreis (2013), http://www.meisterkreis-deutschland.com (accessed the 16th March 2013).

Mercedes-Benz (2013), http://www5.mercedes-benz.com/en/zeitgeist/the_avantgarde_diaries_en/ (accessed the 1st May 2013).

Michau, R. (2009), Upping the luxury quotient with art, http://luxurysociety.com/articles/2009/03/upping-the-luxury-quotient-with-art (accessed the 23rd December 2012).

Millward Brown (2012), Luxury. Feeling entitled, consumers spent on luxury goods, http://www.millwardbrown.com/BrandZ/Top_100_Global_Brands/Previous_Years_Results/2012/Categories/Luxury.aspx (accessed the 15th March 2013).

Mojena, R. (1977), Hierarchical grouping methods and stopping rules. An evaluation, in: The Computer Journal, Vol. 20, No. 4, pp. 359-363.

Montblanc (2013), Lang Lang et la Fondation Culturelle Montblanc, http://www.montblanc.com/fr-fr/flash/default.aspx/#/meet-montblanc/arts-and-culture?music-3612714478439017287/lang-lang-and-the-montblanc-cultural-foundation-8566847645980450034 (accessed the 27th June 2013).

Morris, J. (1971), Warum ist das Kunst? Eine illustrierte Einführung in das Kunstverständnis, in die Moderne Kunst und die zeitgenössischen Stile, Munich.

Mortelmans, D. (2005), Sign values in processes of distinction. The concept of luxury, in: Semiotica, Vol. 157, No. 1-4, pp. 497-520.

Mousse Magazine (2011), Danh Vo at Kunsthalle Fridericianum, http://moussemagazine.it/danh-vo-at-kunsthalle-fridericianum-kassel/#more-14052 (accessed the 7th June 2013).

Mühlmann, H. (1975), Luxus und Komfort. Wortgeschichte und Wortvergleich, Bonn.

Mulier, T. (2012), Richemont to acquire Peter Millar, U.S. luxury sportswear brand, http://www.bloomberg.com/news/2012-09-21/richemont-to-acquire-peter-millar-u-s-luxury-sportswear-brand.html (accessed the 2nd May 2013).

Nehb, J. (2013), Fucking James Franco, http://www.kunst-magazin.de/fucking-james-franco/ (accessed the 21st April 2013).

Neville, S./Cochrane, L. (2013), Shock over departure of creative director behind Mulberry's rise to top, http://www.guardian.co.uk/fashion/2013/jun/10/mulberry-creative-director-emma-hill-quits (accessed the 12th June 2013).

Nueno, J. L./Quelch, J. A. (1998), The mass marketing of luxury, in: Business Horizons, Vol. 41, No. 6, pp. 61-68.

Nufer, G. (2007), Event-Marketing und –Management. Theorie und Praxis unter besonderer Berücksichtigung von Imagewirkungen, 3rd edition, Wiesbaden.

Nufer, G. (2012), Event-Marketing und –Management. Grundlagen – Planung – Wirkungen – Weiterentwicklungen, 4th edition, Wiesbaden.

Oberauer, K./Hörnig, R./Weidenfeld, A./Wilhelm, O. (2005), Effects of directionality in deductive reasoning. II. Premise integration and conclusion evaluation, in: Quarterly Journal of Experimental Psychology: Section A., Vol. 58, No. 7, pp. 1225-1247.

O'Donovan (2011), The Max Mara art prize for women, http://www.whitechapelgallery.org/projects/prizes (accessed the 29th June 2013).

Okonkwo, U. (2007), Luxury fashion branding. Trends, tactics, techniques, Hampshire/New York.

OMA (2013), http://www.oma.eu/projects/2001/prada-new-york (accessed the 25th April 2013).

Opitz, O. (1980), Numerische Taxonomie, Stuttgart/New York.

Osborne, R./Sturgis, D./Turner, N. (2012), Kunsttheorie für Einsteiger, Munich.

Pak, R. (2011), Kongo graffiti for Hermès Scotts Square store, http://fashionslop.wordpress.com/2011/11/21/kongo-graffiti-for-hermes-scotts-square-store/ (accessed the 7th June 2013).

Pallach, U.-C. (1987), Materielle Kultur und Mentalitäten im 18. Jahrhundert, Munich.

Pantazi, C. (2013), The fashion industry's 10 most eccentric designers, http://flavorwire.com/365257/the-fashion-industrys-10-most-eccentric-designers (accessed the 2nd April 2013).

Parry, R. (2008), Episteme and techne, http://plato.stanford.edu/entries/episteme-techne/ (accessed the 18th February 2013).

Pennino, G. (2013), The capsule collection, http://www.vogue.it/en/encyclo/fashion/c/capsule-collection (accessed the 28th December 2012).

Petersen, A. (2008), Art-Kommerz. Kunst und Mode sind eine gute Partie, http://www.welt.de/lifestyle/article2869221/Kunst-und-Mode-sind-eine-gute-Partie.html (accessed the 29th June 2013).

Phau, I./Prendergast, G. (2000), Consuming luxury brands. The relevance of the 'rarity principle', in: Journal of Brand Management, Vol. 8, No. 2, pp. 122 - 138.

Pieroth, B./Schlink, B. (2012), Grundrechte. Staatsrecht II, 28th edition, Heidelberg.

Popper, K. R. (1971), Logik der Forschung, 4th edition, Tübingen.

Povoledo, E. (2012), Art and fashion rub elbows, http://www.nytimes.com/2012/04/26/arts/art-and-fashion-rub-elbows.html?pagewanted=all (accessed the 27th December 2012).

Presseportal (2011), Leica Camera AG zum Mitglied des Comité Colbert ernannt, http://www.presseportal.de/pm/16956/2071945/leica-camera-ag-zum-mitglied-des-comit-colbert-ernannt-mit-bild (accessed the 16th March 2013).

Proctor, R. A. (2009), The evolving marriage of art and fashion, http://luxurysociety.com/articles/2009/04/the-evolving-marriage-of-art-and-fashion (accessed the 23rd December 2012).

Radon, A. (2012), Luxury brand exclusivity strategies. An illustration of cultural collaboration, in: Journal of Business Administration Research, Vol. 1, No. 1, pp. 106-110.

Regier, S./Bulut, C. (2012), Co-Branding als strategische Option der Luxusmarkenführung. Eine empirische Untersuchung, Lohmar.

Rich Jade (2013), http://www.richjade.com/ (accessed the 25th April 2013).

Ringe, C. (2009), Marken als Partner von Künstlern. Wie sich Glaubwürdigkeit auf den Imagetransfer auswirkt, in: Kulturmanagement, Vol. 35, No. 9, pp. 25-27.

Rips, L. J. (2001), Two kinds of reasoning, in: Psychological Science, Vol. 12, No. 2, pp. 129-134.

Rupert Sanderson (2012), Margot Bowman's art attack on Rupert Sanderson, http://www.rupertsanderson.com/hk/press/press-releases/margot-bowman's-art-attack-on-rupert-sanderson.html (accessed the 7th June 2013).

Saatchi, C. (2011), Charles Saatchi. The hideousness of the art world, http://www.guardian.co.uk/commentisfree/2011/dec/02/saatchi-hideousness-art-world (accessed the 29th March 2013).

Saltz, J. (2007), Deal or no deal, http://nymag.com/arts/art/reviews/32367/ (accessed the 5th July 2013).

Schlittgen, R. (1996), Statistische Inferenz, Munich.

Schmidt, A. (2007), Co-Opera – Kooperationen mit Leben füllen. Ein multiperspektivischer Blick auf die Entwicklung von Unternehmenskooperationen innerhalb von Clustern und Netzwerken, Heidelberg.

Schmücker, R. (1998), Was ist Kunst? Eine Grundlegung, Munich.

Schögel, M. (2006), Kooperationsfähigkeiten im Marketing. Eine empirische Untersuchung, Wiesbaden.

Schögel, M./Tomczak, T. (2009), Fallstudie, in: Baumgarth, C./Eisend, M./ Evanschitzky, H. (2009, Eds), Empirische Mastertechniken. Eine anwendungsorientierte Einführung für die Marketing- und Managementforschung, Wiesbaden, pp. 77-105.

Scholz, R. (2013), Art. 5 GG, in: Maunz, T./Dürig, G. (2013, Eds), Grundgesetz-Kommentar. Loseblattsammlung, 67th edition, Munich.

Schwaiger, M./Sarstedt, M./Taylor, C. (2010), Art for sake of the corporation. Audi, BMW Group, DaimlerChrysler, Montblanc, Siemens, and Volkswagen help explore the effect of sponsorship on corporate reputations, in: Journal of Advertising Research, Vol. 50, No. 1, pp. 77-90.

Scott, T. (2010), A brief introduction to the "traditional doctrine of art", in: Fabbri, R./ Scott, T. (2010, Eds), Vincit omnia veritas. Collected essays, Bendigo, pp. 71-78.

Sherman, L. (2008), World's most powerful luxury brands, http://www.forbes.com/ 2008/05/08/style-brands-powerful-forbeslife-cx_ls_0508style.html (accessed the 15th March 2013).

Shiner, L. (2003), The invention of art. A cultural history, Chicago.

Siegle, L. (2012), Is H&M the new home of ethical fashion?, http://www.guardian. co.uk/business/2012/apr/07/hennes-mauritz-h-and-m (accessed the 9th February 2013).

Silverlining (2013), http://www.silverliningfurniture.co.uk/ (accessed the 20th May 2013).

Silverstein, M. J./Fiske, N. (2005), Trading up. Why consumers want new luxury goods and how companies create them, 2nd edition, New York.

Sodeur, W. (1974), Empirische Verfahren zur Klassifikation, Stuttgart.

Sombart, W. (1967), Liebe, Luxus und Kapitalismus, Munich.

Sowray, B. (2012), Maison Martin Margiela and Alexis Mabille awarded haute couture status, http://fashion.telegraph.co.uk/news-features/TMG9757460/Maison-Martin-Margiela-and-Alexis-Mabille-awarded-haute-couture-status.html (accessed the 2nd May 2013).

Stecker, R. (2002), Warum wir nach einer Definition der Kunst suchen sollten, in: Bluhm, R./Schmücker, R. (2002, Eds), Kunst und Kunstbegriff. Der Streit um die Grundlagen der Ästhetik, Paderborn, pp. 118-139.

Steinhausen, D./Langer, K. (1977), Clusteranalyse. Einführung in Methoden und Verfahren der automatischen Klassifikation, Berlin/New York.

Stelzner, J. (2012), Leo Kuelbs für Dom Pérignon, http://blog.interview.de/Leo-Kuelbs-fur-Dom-Perignon (accessed the 28th December 2012).

Stollsteiner, M. (2008), Das A.R.T.-Prinzip. Vom Nutzen der Kunst im Unternehmen, Wiesbaden.

Swengley, N. (2011), Artists add lustre to luxury brands, http://www.theartnews paper.com/articles/Artists-add-lustre-to-luxury-brands/25263 (accessed the 27th December 2012).

Sydow, J. (1992), Strategische Netzwerke. Evolution und Organisation, Wiesbaden.

Sydow, J. (2010a), Über Netzwerke, Allianzsysteme, Verbünde, Kooperationen und Konstellationen, in: Sydow, J. (2010, Ed.), Management von Netzwerk-organisationen. Beiträge aus der „Managementforschung“, 5th edition, Wiesbaden, pp. 1-6.

Sydow, J. (2010b), Management von Netzwerkorganisationen – Zum Stand der Forschung, in: Sydow, J. (2010, Ed.), Management von Netzwerkorganisationen. Beiträge aus der „Managementforschung“, 5th edition, Wiesbaden, pp. 373-470.

Tan, P.-N./Steinbach, M./Kumar, V. (2005), Introduction to data mining, Boston.

Teichmann, S. (2000), Unternehmenstheater zur Unterstützung von Veränderungs-prozessen, Wiesbaden.

The Avant/Garde Diaries (2013), http://www.theavantgardediaries.com/ (accessed the 1st May 2013).

The Economist (1993), The luxury-good trade, Issue from 26th December 1992 – 8th January 1993, pp. 91-94.

The Observer (2003), Is fashion a true art form?, http://www.guardian.co.uk/ artanddesign/2003/jul/13/art.artsfeatures1 (accessed the 2nd April 2013).

Tietz, B. (1960), Bildung und Verwendung von Typen in der Betriebswirtschaftslehre. Dargelegt am Beispiel der Typologie der Messen und Ausstellungen, Cologne/ Opladen.

Topping, L. (2012), The face of fashion: Creative director, http://flaneur.me.uk/01/creative-directors-the-face-of-fashion/ (accessed the 18th March 2013).

Torres, L./Kamhi, M. M. (2000), What art is: The esthetic theory of Ayn Rand, Illinois.

Tribe, M./Jana, R. (2006), New media art, Berlin.

Trochim, W. M. (2006), The research methods knowledge base, http://www.socialresearchmethods.net/kb (accessed the 1st April 2013).

Tungate, M. (2009), Luxury world. The past, present and future of luxury brands, London.

Ullrich, W. (2006), Was war Kunst. Biographien eines Begriffs, 2nd edition, Frankfurt on the Main.

Valtin, A. (2005), Der Wert von Luxusmarken. Determinanten des konsumorientierten Markenwerts und Implikationen für das Luxusmarkenmanagement, Wiesbaden.

Vanhamme, J./Lindgreen, A./Reast, J./Popering, N. (2012), To do well by doing good. Improving corporate image through cause-related marketing, in: Journal of Business Ethics, Vol. 109, No. 3, pp. 259-274.

Varadarajan, P. R./Menon, A. (1988), Cause-related marketing. A coalignment of marketing strategy and corporate philanthropy, in: Journal of Marketing, Vol. 52, No. 3, pp. 58-74.

Veblen, T. (1934), The theory of the leisure class. An economic study of institutions, New York.

Vickers, J. (2013), The problem of induction, http://plato.stanford.edu/archives/spr2013/entries/induction-problem/ (accessed the 1st April 2013).

Vickers, J. S./Renand, F. (2003), The marketing of luxury goods. An exploratory study – Three conceptual dimensions, in: The Marketing Review, Vol. 3, No. 4, pp. 459-478.

Vigneron, F./Johnson, L. W. (1999), A review and a conceptual framework of prestige-seeking consumer behavior, in: Academy of Marketing Science Review (online), Vol. 1.

Vigneron, F./Johnson, L. W. (2004), Measuring perceptions of brand luxury, in: Journal of Brand Management, Vol. 11, No. 6, pp. 484 - 506.

Vogel, F. (1975), Probleme und Verfahren der numerischen Klassifikation, Göttingen.

Vukelic, S. (2000), Unternehmensidentität als Ressource. Zur Bedeutung eines identitätsorientierten Ressourcenmanagements für die Luxusgüterindustrie, Wiesbaden.

Walpole (2013), http://www.thewalpole.co.uk/ (accessed the 15th March 2013).

Wellhöfer, P. R. (1984), Grundstudium sozialwissenschaftliche Methoden und Arbeitsweisen. Eine Einführung für Sozialwissenschaftler und Sozialarbeiter/-pädagogen, Stuttgart.

Wiedmann, K.-P./Hennigs, N./Siebels, A. (2007), Measuring consumers' luxury value perception. A cross-cultural framework, in: Academy of Marketing Science Review (online), Vol. 7.

Winter, K. (2009), Wirkungen von Limited Editions für Marken. Theoretische Überlegungen und empirische Überprüfungen, Wiesbaden.

Witt, M. (2012), Art: Legendary graffiti artist Futura crafts limited edition bottle for Hennessy, http://www.strictlysocial.com/2012/art-futura-hennessy-limited-edition-bottle/ (accessed the 30th April 2013).

World Luxury Brand Directory (2013), http://www.conceptofluxurybrands.com/world_luxury_brand_directory (accessed the 17th March 2013).

Yin, R. K. (2009), Case study research. Design and methods, 4th edition, Thousand Oaks.

Zhao, B. (2010), Lacoste launches porcelain polo shirts by Li Xiaofeng, http://fr.blouinartinfo.com/news/story/35197/lacoste-launches-porcelain-polo-shirts-by-li-xiaofeng (accessed the 30th April 2013).

List of appendices

I. Data bases

II. Sample demographics

III. Attribute selection

IV. Cluster analysis

MIX
Papier aus verantwortungsvollen Quellen
Paper from responsible sources
FSC® C105338

If you have any concerns about our products,
you can contact us on
ProductSafety@springernature.com

In case Publisher is established outside the EU,
the EU authorized representative is:
Springer Nature Customer Service Center GmbH
Europaplatz 3, 69115 Heidelberg, Germany

Printed by Libri Plureos GmbH
in Hamburg, Germany